Sondra's Search

ESTER KATZ SILVERS

DEVORA
PUBLISHING
JERUSALEM ◆ NEW YORK

Sondra's Search
Published by Devora Publishing Company
Text Copyright © 2007 by Ester Katz Silvers

COVER DESIGN: Benjie Herskowitz
TYPESETTING & BOOK DESIGN: Jerusalem Typesetting
EDITOR: Shirley Zauer
EDITORIAL & PRODUCTION MANAGER: Daniella Barak

Hard Cover ISBN: 978-1-932687-95-8

E-MAIL: sales@devorapublishing.com
WEB SITE: www.devorapublishing.com

Printed in Israel

To my family

Contents

Apfelbaum Family Tree

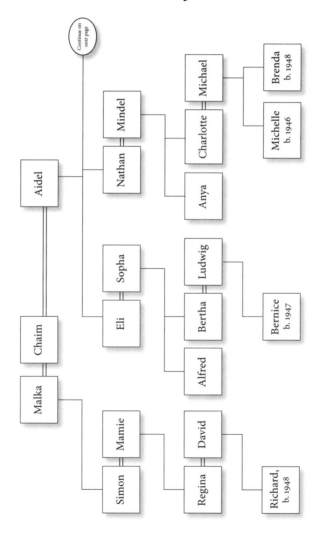

Continue on next page

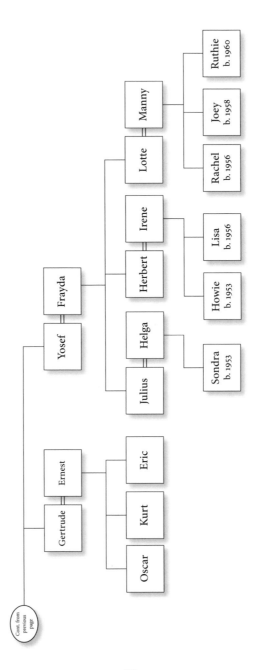

Prologue

As the plane from Israel began its gradual descent, the stewardess made her announcements, first in English and then in German, Danny Klein closed his *gemara*, tightened his seat belt, and rearranged his suede *yarmulke* on his unruly brown hair. He smiled somewhat nervously at Sondra Apfelbaum, his seatmate and fiancee of a month.

"Excited?"

She, oblivious to his smile, had her face pressed against the plastic window, eyes glued to the countryside. Below her were the majestic Alps, unbelievably green to her eyes after almost a year in Israel. This was the land of Grimm's fairy tales, Heidi, and her parents' birthplace. This was the land of her mission, the place she and her cousin had once vowed to come and find the missing Torah scroll. This was the land whose history had set her on her search to find true meaning in Judaism.

Full of emotion, she peeled her dark eyes from the window and turned to Danny.

"Isn't it beautiful?" she whispered.

"Yes," Danny agreed reluctantly, "but look down there at the train tracks."

"What?" Sondra asked, puzzled.

"I wonder if those were tracks to the concentration camps?"

"Oh, Danny," Sondra said reproachfully.

"Sorry, sorry," Danny said hastily. "Forget I said that."

Sondra again turned her head to the window, but now her eyes were full of unshed tears. It was more the mention of the train tracks than the camps that made her lips quiver. She closed her eyes and again, for the millionth time, pictured that horrible photo from the paper's front page. As if it were in front of her, she could still see the mangled Jaguar, the Santa Fe freight car, the rescue workers, all against the background of a cloudy, midnight, Kansas sky. She gave an involuntary shudder. It had happened three years ago, a lifetime ago, but sometimes it was as painful as the first time she saw it.

"Sondra," Danny's voice broke into her thoughts, "I'm really sorry I said anything about the concentration camps."

"Oh," Sondra bit her lower lip, resolutely put her memories away, and turned to the earnest young man. "I'm sorry, I didn't mean to turn my back on you. I was just lost in my thoughts, but I'm back to the present now," she smiled, the dimple in her left cheek deepening.

"Are you excited?"

Sondra nodded, her black ponytail bobbing behind her. "This is like a dream come true for me. I can't believe it all fell into place and we were able to get the connection home by way of Frankfort."

"I can't believe your mother never told you anything about her experiences in the Holocaust."

"She was always silent on the subject. I sure hope I'll understand her better after this trip."

"I know," Danny nodded sympathetically. He clasped his hands tightly as the plane touched ground. Silently he prayed that their stop in Germany would indeed be a dream come true and not a nightmare.

Chapter One

When the lunch bell rang at Lincoln Elementary School, eleven-year-old Sondra had no idea that during the next hour her life was going to change forever. She waved good-bye to her classmates as she climbed aboard her father's mud-spattered pick-up truck that was standing in front of the school waiting for her.

"Hi, Daddy," she leaned over and gave her father a kiss. His clean-shaven face was smooth and he was dressed in a blue suit that matched his eyes. That was the way he dressed every weekday when he worked in the Men's Department at Apple's Department Store. It was quite a contrast to the father Sondra saw in the morning when she woke up and in the evening before supper. Then he would be dressed in old, ragged work clothes with a woolen cap on his head and high rubber boots on his feet. Sometimes Sondra kept him company in the barn while he milked the dozen dairy cows by hand. Once in a while, when it wasn't too cold, she still helped him. It was one of their special times together.

Julius Apfelbaum drove his truck five blocks out of town and then rode over a narrow bridge and around potholes for a tenth of a mile until they arrived home. Home was a two-story farmhouse set on seventy acres of rich, Kansas pastureland. Waiting at the back porch was Helga. A small woman, with short, black hair and dark eyes, it was clear that Sondra got her looks from her mother.

Helga's face lit up at the sight of her daughter and husband and she had a kiss for both of them. Sondra returned the kiss with a smile and the dimple on her left cheek deepened.

"What's for dinner?" Sondra asked as she entered the sunny kitchen. With red gingham wallpaper, lacy white curtains, and a bright, white, old-fashioned gas stove it was a most cheerful room. In the summers the family ate their meals in the dark dining room full of ornate furniture and china knickknacks that had been brought over from Germany. It was wasteful, though, in the winter to heat that room just for mealtimes.

As Sondra sat down to the pot roast her mother had made she felt sorry for all her other classmates, who were sitting down to a cold peanut butter or lunchmeat sandwich with only their mothers for company. It was her father with his funny stories from work who made their meals lively. She and her mother were an appreciative audience, and often one of her father's stories would remind her mother of an amusing anecdote from college. There was usually a lot of laughter at the table.

This meal, though, Sondra had something on her mind. An assignment for science, making a family tree to study the similarities between the children, parents, and grandparents, had reminded her that she had no idea what her maternal grandparents looked like. Dipping her bread into her gravy, she took a deep breath.

"How come we don't have any pictures of Mommy's family?"

There was a silence and Sondra heard her mother, suddenly pale, set her fork down.

"I..., I don't feel well. I think I will lie down."

Sondra watched as her mother made her way from the table. Sondra suddenly felt uncomfortable, and angry that she felt that way.

"What happened?" she asked her father with an edge to her voice.

Julius Apfelbaum wiped his hands and mouth methodically

and set the linen napkin next to his plate. He rubbed his hand across his eyes and moved his chair closer to his daughter.

"Do you remember last fall when Cousin Oscar told you how his parents were killed by Hitler?"

"Yes," Sondra nodded her head slowly, feeling fearful.

"The same thing happened to Mommy's parents." Julius reached out and took his daughter's hand.

"I don't understand," the little girl said. "Mommy always tells me such nice stories about her parents."

"It was nice, 'til Hitler came to power."

"Why didn't her parents leave like Oma and Opa?"

"My parents had great-uncle Simon here to help them. Mommy's family had nowhere to go. Listen, Sondra," Julius closed his daughter's smooth, little hands inside his two callused ones. "The Nazis made my life hard. I had to leave home and start over again here in America. But that is nothing like what happened to Mommy. They murdered her parents and her little sister. Mommy had to work in a work camp and was a slave. I know very little about it because Mommy does not want to talk about it. It hurts her too much. Any questions you have you can ask me, but not Mommy. Do you understand?"

Sondra nodded her head slowly. "The Nazis burned the pictures, right." It was a statement, not a question and the tears that had been threatening to overflow ever since her mother left the table broke into heartrending sobs. Her Daddy put his arms around her and patted her back, but he did not say everything would be all right as he usually did. He let her cry herself out and then, once she had dried her face, suggested they have dessert.

"How can you think of dessert?" Sondra accused her father with resentful eyes.

He shocked her by laughing quietly. "Sweetheart," he said, stroking her dark hair, "I know this is hard for you, but I've had twenty years to come to terms with everything the Nazis did to us. The best revenge I can take is to live a normal life and show them that they didn't kill all of us."

5

In the end, Sondra ate the bowl of applesauce her father brought her. The two of them cleaned up the kitchen together and Sondra was just a little late going back to school. If anyone in the sixth grade class noticed that she had been crying, they did not mention it.

She was surprised when she returned home that afternoon to find her mother sitting at the kitchen table with her history textbooks spread out in front of her as if nothing unusual had happened that noon. Helga chatted pleasantly with her daughter while Sondra ate an apple. If she had not known better, Sondra would have thought she had imagined the whole thing.

"I think I'll ride my bike over to Howie's," Sondra announced.

Helga nodded her approval. "If you're going to be late, ride over to the store and Daddy can put your bike in the back of the truck and bring you home." She kissed her daughter good-bye and watched from the window as Sondra took her green Schwinn out of the barn and pedaled out of sight.

Howie lived across town, past the university, in the newer section of Lincoln. Their fathers were brothers and the two cousins were born a month apart. Sondra's earliest memories were of Uncle Herbert dropping off Aunt Irene at the farmhouse so she and Howie could play together while their mothers visited. In Sondra's eyes, it was a tragedy that they went to different grammar schools, but it was probably one of the best things for Sondra. Quite a daydreamer, she tended to look to Howie for direction when they were together. Being in different schools had made her more independent.

Aunt Irene answered the door. As far as Sondra was concerned, her aunt was one of the prettiest women she had ever seen. Slim and stylish with her honey-blonde hair twisted into a French knot, she was quite a contrast to Helga. Sondra's mother cared little about clothing other than that it was clean and comfortable. Still Irene and Helga were the best of friends, talking to each other daily.

"How are you, Sondra?" Irene asked.

"Okay," Sondra answered, hoping that her aunt had not noticed her swollen eyes. She wondered when the family had all switched languages. German had been Sondra's mother tongue, but now she spoke English with everyone but her Oma.

Irene ushered her into the modern, electric kitchen where Howie and Lisa were. Lisa was dressed in her Blue Bird's uniform, complete with the girls' club beanie. She and Howie were just finishing bowls of ice cream. Irene left the children and returned to her ironing in the basement. Indeed, she had noticed Sondra's swollen eyes. She had called Helga that afternoon, not long after the kids had gone back to school. In a strained voice her sister-in-law had said she had a headache and didn't feel like talking. Helga called back an hour later and was her normal, cheerful self. Still, Irene did not need to be a psychologist to know that there was a connection between Sondra's swollen eyes and Irene's headache.

With an impatient motion Irene ran the iron back and forth across Herbert's handkerchiefs. As much as she loved her sister-in-law, Irene strongly felt that she did not belong in a small town with only a handful of Jews and no other Holocaust survivors. Irene had been fourteen when her family left Germany, but that had been in 1936 before things got really bad. They had moved to Omaha, where her father had an aunt. Irene had learned English and made friends quickly. She had none of the horrible memories that haunted Helga. Nor did the rest of the family, all of whom had gotten out in time.

As much as she would miss her, Irene thought Julius should sell his cows, quit working for Uncle Simon, and take his family to live in Kansas City where Helga would find friends with similar backgrounds. But Uncle Simon would never approve and Julius would never go against his wishes. Thank goodness Herbert had stopped working at the store as soon as he finished high school.

Raising cattle was hard work and Herbert put in many ten- and twelve-hour days, but at least he was his own boss.

Meanwhile, back in the kitchen Sondra had refused Howie's offer of ice cream. She bided her time, waiting for Lisa to leave for her Blue Bird meeting. The eight-year-old finished her last drop of ice cream and ran out.

"What's wrong?" Howie asked. He was a big boy for his eleven years, broad-shouldered and tall.

Without preamble Sondra explained what she has learned at lunch.

"Wow," Howie exclaimed, "I didn't know that!"

"Nobody talks about it. My mother doesn't like to talk about it."

"Oscar doesn't like to talk about it either."

"I know," Sondra answered sadly. "But I want to know what happened to Mommy's parents!"

Howie leaned back in his chair so that only two legs remained on the floor. He rested his blonde head against the wall and studied his cousin.

"You know," he tried to be comforting, "a lot of kids our age don't have any grandparents. At least, you have Oma. Try not to think about it."

"*Try not to think about it!*" Sondra exclaimed. "You wouldn't be saying that if it were your grandparents."

"Don't get into a tiff," Howie sat straight in his chair. "There's no point worrying about something you can't change. "Do you want to look at my new rock star magazine?"

"No," Sondra answered shortly. Last year she and Howie had spent hours sitting together reading comic books. Now he was just interested in sports and rock star magazines. She could not understand what everyone saw in the Beatles. "I'm going to the library."

"Do you want me to come with you?"

"If you want."

Howie followed her out of the house and jumped on his new ten-speed. As they pedaled side by side, they made a handsome pair. He, with his Nordic good looks, was quite a contrast to his dark little cousin. Once inside the library, Howie picked up a *Sports Illustrated* and Sondra made her way to the card catalogue. It was the first time she had used it. Normally she would browse through the fiction section and grab books whose titles interested her. This time she looked up two subjects, Nazi and Holocaust. After wandering through the shelves she came to the librarian's desk with two books. One was an elementary World War II history and the other was *The Diary of Anne Frank*.

The librarian pointed to the second book. "You might find this a little difficult, Sondra."

"I want to try," the girl insisted.

"Okay," the woman said as she stamped the books.

The two cousins parted on the library steps and Sondra rode home to delve into her books. She made no mention of them to her mother, but when she did have questions she turned to her father, her Oma, or sometimes even to Cousin Oscar. Soon the librarian realized what subject Sondra was interested in and guided her to find books that were on her level.

Summer came with its ninety-degree-plus weather and the pool opened. Howie gave Sondra no peace every morning until she agreed to meet him at The Crystal Plunge. She never suspected that he had received directions from his parents to keep her out of her room and in the sunshine. Although she was uncomfortable to be seen in a bathing suit with her budding new shape, it was fun frolicking in the water. And Howie was more like the old Howie, talking far less about rock groups and far more about fishing, baseball, and cookouts. Sondra continued her reading, but she learned that she could still enjoy life, even if the Nazis had murdered her grandparents. By the time she entered seventh grade at the junior high school, she had developed a maturity that impressed her teachers.

Chapter Two

Junior high had been an adjustment for Sondra. The students from Lincoln's three grammar schools all came together under one roof, and she was chagrined to find herself sitting in classrooms where she did not know even half the kids. By the time winter break came, though, she had found her place as one of the better students and had been asked to serve on the newspaper staff. Also among the crew was Jane Tucker, whose father was a minister. Petite like Sondra, she had curly, blonde hair that she was always playing with. As vivacious as Sondra was self-contained, the two girls shared a love of books, learning, and daydreams. They became good friends.

Howie had also found his place. As a talented basketball player he immediately became part of the cool crowd. He was still the same Howie, but some of the things Sondra noticed his friends doing bothered her. When she saw a couple of them making fun of Sammy Borden, one of the special-education students, she decided to mention it to her cousin.

"Oh, Sondra, they didn't mean anything by it," Howie remonstrated. "Charlie likes the attention."

"I don't think so," Sondra shook her head. "They ended up taking some money from him, too."

"So what do you want me to do about it?"

"Talk to them."

"Like they're going to listen to me." Howie's voice was sarcastic.

"Why not?" Sondra was perfectly serious.

Howie made a face. "I'm not a preacher. I'm just one of the kids."

"Okay," Sondra could not hide her disappointment in her cousin and he was stung by her unspoken criticism. There was a subtle coolness between the two cousins for the next couple of days. It could have gone on forever if Aunt Irene hadn't had her annual Hanukkah party.

Aunt Irene had it every year on Sunday, when the store was closed and no one could claim they had to work. All the family in Lincoln would come. This year Sondra was thrilled that her cousin, Bernice, was home from Oklahoma University for the weekend and would stay for the gathering. It always began with candle lighting and then came the food – latkes, chopped liver, various salads, and kugels. The emphasis was definitely on food and there had never been a gift exchange. This year there was a break in that tradition.

"I've eaten more than was good for me," Oscar rose abruptly from his chair before the Hanukkah lights had burned down. "Are you ready, Uncle Simon?"

The old gentleman shook his head. "You go ahead. Berta will take me home, right?"

Cousin Berta nodded her head. It had been more of a command than a question.

Before walking out the door, Oscar gruffly handed out envelopes to Howie, Lisa, Bernice, and Sondra. He left quickly before they could open them.

Howie was the first to tear his open and was startled to see a check inside.

"Fifteen hundred dollars!" the boy exclaimed.

"Let me see that," Herbert grabbed the check out of his son's hand.

Immediately the girls opened their envelopes and found checks for the same amount.

Dumbfounded, Julius raced outside to try and catch his cousin, but Oscar was already gone. He returned to the living room and a babble of excitement.

"Where did he get all that money from?"

"Can I buy a car?"

"Think what he could do with all that money."

"Isn't that just like Oscar. Hand out a small fortune and not stay to get thanked."

"It's money from Germany," Uncle Simon spoke up from the easy chair he was reclining in. "Oscar doesn't want it."

With his cryptic explanation, the adults all began discussing their experiences with the endless forms they had filled out in order to receive their reparations money. Sondra did not know if she was the only one to notice her mother's stillness and pale face, but after a few minutes Helga reached out and pulled at Julius's arm. Quickly her father stood up.

"Well, Irene, it was delicious, but I have to get up early tomorrow and milk those cows." He spoke jovially as usual and made his rounds saying good night. Helga said little to anyone and the short ride home was a silent one.

Later when he thought Sondra was upstairs in bed, Julius carefully broached the subject again.

"You know, you're entitled to more money than I received. Don't you think we should open a file?"

"The money can't bring the dead back to life," Helga snapped. "Why should I help the Nazis ease their consciences?"

"There's a lot we could do with the money," Julius spoke softly.

"I … I don't want to talk about it," Helga retreated into silence as she always did when anything to do with the Holocaust was mentioned.

Thirsty from all the liver and latkes, Sondra had come down the stairs to get a drink. She stopped on the last step, not fully understanding the conversation, but knowing she was not supposed to have overheard it. Silently she went back up the stairs, ignoring her thirst. The dialogue between her parents was not forgotten, but stored in her memory to puzzle over from time to time.

The next morning Howie couldn't wait to talk about the money. The excitement of the gifts had broken the coolness between the two of them. Sondra listened patiently to what kind of car Howie wanted to buy. Her check would lie in the bank collecting interest for her college education. The two cousins agreed that they would not tell anyone at school about their gift.

Comfortable with their agreement and shared secret, both were careful not to cause another rift. Sondra resolved to try not to criticize her cousin. Howie decided that if some of the cool kids wanted to act like jerks, that was their business, but he would be extra careful not to copy them. The two of them were able to stick to their resolutions – for a while.

Chapter Three

*S*ondra was bored. School had been out for a month. Jane was on vacation. Howie was busy studying for his *bar mitzvah*. Helga was writing a paper. There was nothing interesting on TV. The Crystal Plunge was closed. It hadn't opened at all in protest against the government's integration order. Julius and Helga, who remembered well what it had been like to be barred from public places because they were Jewish, were all for letting Afro-Americans and whites swim together. Sondra really didn't care; she just wanted the pool to be open. She had finished her last book and was tired of reading. In desperation she decided to visit her Oma.

Frayda Apfelbaum was a short, stocky woman, but somehow she carried herself with grace. Even if she was just at home, puttering about in her kitchen, her white hair was always neatly brushed, tied into a bun with the short wisps of hair caught back with her tortoiseshell combs. Although she kept busy with her fine handiwork, baking, and correspondence, the little two-bedroom farmhouse where she lived seemed awfully big ever since her husband, Josef, had died three years earlier.

"Sondra, how are you, dear?" Frayda was thrilled to have a visitor. "I just took some butter cookies out of the oven."

"Great!" Sondra smiled, revealing the dimple in her left cheek.

As the two settled down at the oak table in the dining room, Frayda picked up her knitting. "Are you enjoying your vacation?"

"I guess so," Sondra shrugged. "What are you making?"

"A sweater for Lisa for the bar mitzvah. I want to make one for you, too."

"Thank you. What about Rachel and Ruthie?" Sondra asked about her cousins in Kansas City.

"Of course," her Oma answered. "They're after you. If I have time I'll make one for myself, too."

"You'll have time," Sondra laughed, knowing how quickly her grandmother worked. "It's not for another four months."

"Yes," Frayda nodded, "it will be nice to see someone really read from the Torah and not just from a book laid on top of it as usual."

There was no rabbi in Lincoln and no synagogue. When the family had first come to Kansas from Germany they had held weekly services in Uncle Simon's spacious living room. That had been when all of the cousins had lived there and all of the uncles were still alive. By the time Sondra was born, there were not enough men for a *minyan*, a quorum of ten men. The family would drive to Wichita to attend services from time to time and always on the High Holidays. Then, two years ago, there had been a surge in the number of Jewish students enrolled at the university. Dr. Cohen, a professor of history and a family friend, had suggested that they organize Rosh Hashanah services at the university chapel.

The Torah scroll and makeshift Ark had been brought over from Uncle Simon's house. One of the students happened to have a *shofar* that his grandparents had brought back for him from their trip to Israel. Cousin Oscar led the services and Dr. Cohen gave the sermon. It had been a success, as had been the Yom Kippur services. The small congregation decided that they would have services once a month on Friday night. Howie would be celebrating the first bar mitzvah, and that would be on Shabbat morning.

"You know," Frayda said, "there is quite a special story about our Sefer Torah."

"Yeah?" Sondra was eager to hear it.

"You should ask Oscar about it."

"Oscar?"

"Yes, Oscar."

"Okay," Sondra agreed. "I'll ask him."

At one time that suggestion would have been terrifying. Sondra and her cousins had always been afraid of Oscar, with his bushy, black eyebrows, scowling face, and stooped shoulders. Then one Sunday afternoon, about two years ago, they had taught him to spit watermelon seeds and he had told them the story of his life. It was a rather pathetic tale of a boy coming of age in a small German village under Nazi rule. Uncle Simon had been able to get him out in 1938, but his parents had waited until it was too late.

Oscar was now Uncle Simon's right hand man in Apple's Department Store, but he had never reconciled himself to American life. After that Sunday, though, a bond had grown between him and his young cousins. Sondra, especially, was fascinated by his stories. Her grandmother's comment made her eager to speak to Oscar, so after finishing the cookies and spending a half-hour weeding in the garden, Sondra decided to go to the store.

Apple's, a two-story edifice half a block long, was the largest store in Lincoln. Sondra's first stop, of course, was the Men's Section, to say hello to her father and his assistant. Cousin Berta waved to her as she passed through the Women's Section and Mrs. Ward greeted her as she skirted the Children's Department. There was no sign of Oscar, so she took the elevator to the second floor. Sure enough, he was in the office with Uncle Simon, talking to a salesman, and had no time for her.

"Typical for the day," Sondra muttered to herself. But by the time she got home Howie had finished his lesson and called to suggest a bike ride to his father's ranch. Once there, Sondra told

Howie all about the conversation she had had with their grandmother. They resolved that, no matter what, they would find the time to ask Oscar about the Torah at Uncle Simon's birthday party.

Simon Apfelbaum had been born in Germany in 1881, but he left when he was barely fourteen years old. He first came to St. Louis, where a cousin had a dry goods store, and worked there for a few years. By the time he was nineteen he wanted to be on his own. Using his hoarded wages, he bought himself a peddler's pack and headed to Nebraska, Kansas, and Indian Territory. He did well and after several years decided to open his own store. Lincoln was a pretty little town without much competition and had an empty store for sale. Rumor had it that a college would be opening there. It was a great opportunity, but before Simon made a final decision, he took a trip back to St. Louis to ask Mamie Oppenheimer to be his wife and settle with him in the little Kansas town.

She agreed and after a few years she and Simon were one of the richest families in Lincoln. They had one daughter, Regina, and she was her parent's pride and joy. She was just twenty when she married David Krauss from New York, who had been studying business at Lincoln State College. After graduation he stayed and worked for his father-in-law. They had a baby boy, Richard, and, despite the Depression, Simon felt that life was good.

He took his family for a trip to Europe and they met all the relatives back in Germany. Everything had been postcard-perfect until the trip home. After two days at sea, Mamie became ill with influenza. When they docked in New York, Simon checked her into the hospital there, but there was nothing to be done for her. She died a week later. As if that were not enough tragedy, Regina was killed in a car accident the following summer. David broke his father-in-law's heart when he decided to leave his memories behind and move back east with his two-year-old son. Although he promised his father-in-law that he would bring the child for yearly visits, Simon was not comforted.

Simon continued to run the store, but his heart was not in it. Although he was apathetic to almost everything, the news about what was going on in Germany began to make an impression on him. He had three brothers, a sister, and all of their families back there. He decided he would bring them all to America, to Lincoln. He would expand the store and help them get a new start in life.

It didn't start out so well. His second brother, Nathan, was appreciative of the help, but his wife, Mindel, had relatives in Chicago. She wanted her two daughters, Anya and Charlotte, to grow up there. Begrudgingly, Simon helped them get settled on the South Side. Two years later Nathan turned to his big brother with financial woes. Simon had been thrilled to offer his brother a job again. The family moved to Lincoln, but it didn't work out. Mindel and Simon just could not get along. Another two years passed and Nathan moved to Winfield, Kansas. He got a job working for a distant, bachelor cousin in his women's apparel store. When the cousin was ready to retire, Nathan bought the business and did well with it. Anya moved back to Chicago as soon as she finished high school, but Charlotte stayed and married the son of the only other Jewish family in town. They had two daughters, Michelle and Brenda. After Mindel died, Simon and Nathan began to get along better, although they would never be close.

With his first brother, Eli, things went better. Eli was eager to come and getting visas for him, his wife, Sopha, and their children, Alfred and Berta, had gone smoothly. Alfred served in the US Army and was killed in action. Berta married a distant cousin, Ludwig, who worked in the store. They had one daughter, Bernice, and she had been just a toddler when her father died of a heart attack. Berta moved back in with her parents and Sopha took care of Bernice while Berta went to work in the women's department at Apple's. Now she was the efficient head of the department. Bernice was studying business at Oklahoma University and spent her summers working in the store. Simon had wanted her to go to Lincoln State, but that was one point he and Berta locked horns on.

"Her chances of getting married in college are big and her chances of finding a Jewish man here in Lincoln are about nil. She's going to Norman, Oklahoma. It's close by and has a good Jewish population."

Simon had not been able to change her mind, but he was looking forward to putting Bernice on staff full time as soon as she graduated.

Frayda, the wife of Simon's youngest brother, Josef, had wanted to leave Germany already in 1933, when Hitler became chancellor. However, Josef dragged his feet. His cattle business was lucrative and he did not want to leave it. Finally, caving in to his wife's nagging and his brother's pleading, he applied for visas for himself, his wife, and their three children, Julius, Herbert, and Lotte. The application was denied; the immigration department claimed that Julius had tuberculosis. That had taken months to clear up and both Simon and Julius were convinced it did only because of a conversation Simon had had with an old friend who was a senator in Washington at that time.

Josef's family had come piecemeal, every six months, beginning with Julius and ending with Frayda and Lotte. Josef bought some land and a little house on the edge of town, and he was content to work his garden and remember his cattle business back in Germany. Simon enrolled the boys in high school and Lotte in the same junior high school that Sondra and Howie now attended. After school they all worked in the store, but Herbert left as soon as he graduated and went into the cattle business, like his father. A cousin from Kansas City invited Lotte for a weekend and introduced her to Manny Katzner, who had an insurance business. Simon tried to talk him into moving the business to Lincoln, but neither Lotte nor Manny liked the idea. They were happy to raise their three children, Rachel, Joey, and Ruthie, in Kansas City, which had its own synagogue. Julius was the only one of Josef's children who followed Simon's plan. Although his dairy business was not doing badly, he still devoted most of his day to the men's department at Apple's.

Simon's only sister, Gertrude, had been a problem. Since her husband had been a decorated hero in World War i, he was convinced that Hitler would not harm them. It was not until 1938 that he finally agreed to send his oldest son out of Germany. Oscar left home a few weeks after the Kristallnacht pogrom in November. Once he had arrived safely and sent letters home begging his family to follow, his father began to think that perhaps they should leave. But by the time he made up his mind, it was too late. Even with all his connections and money, Simon could not get Gertrude, her husband, or her younger sons, Kurt and Eric, out of the country.

Even without knowing any of the stories, Simon's great-nieces and great-nephews thought he was wonderful. A tall, silver-haired man, he was always dressed in a three-piece suit no matter how hot the weather. In the summer his pockets were full of silver dollars and in the winter he put Hershey's chocolate bars in them. Whenever the children shook hands with him they would find themselves holding one of the treats. As they got older, though, they began to sense that some of the adults were not too fond of Simon's patriarchal airs.

Be that as it may, Simon's birthday was coincidentally on the Fourth of July. Every year since he turned sixty, there was always a big party at his home with almost all of the relatives from the area in attendance. This year was no exception and, of course, Richard was there. He always made his yearly visit for his grandfather's birthday. At thirty-six, he was still not married. Supposedly, he spent his time playing with stocks and traveling all over the world. The children looked on him as a glamorous playboy. The adults grumbled that he had never done an honest day's work in his life, while Simon had never stopped working. Still, they were always as anxious to see Richard as to celebrate his grandfather's birthday.

The gossip in Uncle Simon's living room was nonstop and mostly in German. The six young cousins filled their plates with cake and escaped to the wide, circular staircase. Lisa and Rachel shared one step. The two nine-year-old girls were inseparable whenever the Katzners came for a visit. Joey, aged seven, settled himself in between Howie and Sondra, while little Ruthie snuggled up next to Sondra. It was not long before the older cousins, Bernice, Michelle, and Brenda, joined them. Both of the Winfield girls understood only English. They had come to the party as chauffeurs for their grandfather and they were bored with the adults.

Sondra was always thrilled when Bernice chose the children's company over that of the adults. She wished that she felt the same way about Michelle and Brenda, but she did not. There was something about them that made her feel like they were always looking down on her, and Sondra was not sure why. Perhaps they thought they were more American than she was. Sondra thought that was stupid. They should be jealous that she knew two languages. She said a polite hello to them and gave a genuine smile to Bernice.

Tall and big-boned, Bernice was not especially attractive except for her hair and eyes. Since she was twelve years old she had worn her thick, brown hair down to her waist. Sondra had lots of pleasant memories of brushing her cousin's hair while listening to the wonderful stories that Bernice read to her. It was Bernice who had fostered Sondra's love of reading. Whenever the older girl came home she was always interested in what was going on in her cousins' lives. Michelle and Brenda did not share her enthusiasm. They were plainly bored with the discussion about the bar-mitzvah plans.

Brenda made no attempt to stifle a loud yawn, irritating Bernice. She swallowed a nasty comment just as Oscar joined them on the stairs.

"It's too noisy in there," he said shortly and settled himself on the step below the three college girls.

"Oscar, do you want to play hide and seek?" Joey asked his older cousin.

Oscar gave him a puzzled glance. "Don't you think I'm too old for that?"

Joey shrugged. Before he could get too disappointed, though, Lisa and Rachel hailed his idea. With Ruthie in tow the four youngest scrambled up to the third floor where the antique furniture and screened porches made it an excellent playground.

Now was Sondra's chance.

"Oscar," she said after swallowing her last bite of plum kuchen, "Oma says you know a special story about the Torah scroll."

"Well, yes, but you probably would not be interested in it."

"Oh, yes, we would," Howie sat forward.

"Yes," Bernice echoed.

Oscar gave a deep sigh. "It's sad."

"Will it make you feel bad to tell it?" Sondra asked, with a worried frown on her face.

There were a few moments of silence. Sondra, Howie, and Bernice were familiar with Oscar's long silences, but Michelle and Brenda looked decidedly uncomfortable. Finally he spoke.

"I don't want to make you feel bad."

"We won't," Howie answered automatically.

Sondra frowned at him. "Maybe it will make us feel bad," she spoke seriously, "but maybe we'll grow from it."

Oscar smiled at the girl's answer. "Maybe you will."

Bernice whispered a brief history of Oscar's life to Brenda and Michelle while he collected his thoughts.

"I grew up in the same house as your fathers, Sondra and Howie. In Mafdner. Your mother grew up in Frankfort, Bernice, and your family," Oscar turned to the two sisters, "was from another village not too far away. Actually, it wasn't the same house. There was one door and a set of stairs going up to the second floor. We lived on the second floor. My father and Uncle Josef worked together in the cattle business. There were about twenty Jewish families in Mafdner, but by the time the story happened most of them were gone. Your mother's family was left, Sondra, and the Schusters, the Kleins, and us."

Again there was a long silence. "It must have been hard to see so many people leave," Bernice offered.

"*Ja*," Oscar nodded and took up his tale again. "My mother had a friend who wasn't Jewish. Hilda Schmidt was the blacksmith's wife and her son Heinrich was a Nazi." Oscar shook his head in recollection. "He was always a bully, but I don't think he was ever a big Nazi. Like most bullies, he was a coward and he was afraid of his mother, too. He told her that the Kristallnacht was coming."

"What was that?" Howie asked tentatively, embarrassed to expose his ignorance.

"Shh," Sondra nudged him, "it was a giant pogrom all over Germany."

"You're right." Oscar looked at the young girl with obvious respect.

"Well," Oscar sighed, "Mrs. Schmidt told my mother and she told the others about the Kristallnacht and we all went to the forest and hid most of the night. When we finally returned to the village all we did was head to our homes and collapse into our beds. In the morning, though, there was plenty to do. Windows had been broken, furniture smashed, china thrown against the walls."

"It sounds like our neighborhood after the tornado," Brenda interjected.

"This wasn't a tornado," Oscar retorted, "this was Nazis. They searched our homes for valuables they could cart away, but we had taken all of those to the woods with us. Everything of value that was too heavy to take they tried to destroy. My little brother, Kurt, may his blood be avenged, disappeared from the work and I remember my mother was annoyed with him."

"Where did he go?" Howie pushed Oscar on after another long silence.

"To the synagogue. It was in worse shape than the houses. He found the two Torah scrolls on the ground and went home to get his wagon and went back to the shul and brought the Torah scrolls home with him."

"Wasn't he afraid?" Bernice asked. She has heard bits and pieces of the story before but never from Oscar.

Oscar shook his head. "There were no Nazis in the light of day in Mafdner then," he said bitterly.

"And how did the Torah get here?" Sondra prodded.

"They were sending me to Uncle Simon a month later. It was put in my bags. I thought Kurt would use it here for his bar mitzvah, but he never came."

Out from under his bushy eyebrows Oscar glanced at his young cousins and was chagrined to see tears glistening in the girls' eyes. Even Howie was blinking.

"I told you it'd make you feel bad," he almost growled.

Sondra nodded. "But it's important to know. What happened to the other Torah?"

"I don't know."

"You don't know?" Howie exclaimed.

Oscar shook his head. "It was given to the Kleins, but no one knows what happened to them. Your mother, Sondra, was the last one in Mafdner."

They sat in silence a few minutes longer. From upstairs came the sound of laughter and from downstairs the buzz of conversations.

Michelle looked at her watch. "We better get going," she told her sister, "if you're going to be back for your date."

Bernice went down the stairs with them and Oscar decided to return to the adults. Howie turned to Sondra.

"I wonder what happened to the other Torah scroll."

Sondra shook her head.

"Why don't you ask your mother?"

"I can't. Daddy told me I couldn't ask her anything about the war. He said if I had any questions I should ask him."

"So ask him."

"Okay," Sondra agreed. "First chance I get."

Her chance came the next evening during milking. Sondra sat on the cement doorstep of the barn watching her father work. Evening milking was a peaceful time, not like the morning milking.

Then her father would be in a hurry, the radio would be blaring the morning news over the noises of the cows. Traffic would be heavy on the road near the barn. In the evening there were few cars traveling down the road. The cows were tired, willing to be milked and then go to sleep. The air was still. About the only sound Sondra heard was the milk squirting into the metal bucket. She cleared her throat.

"Daddy, what happened to the other Torah that Oscar's brother rescued?"

Julius stopped milking, pulled his handkerchief out of his pocket, wiped his brow, and shook his head. "We don't know."

"You don't?" Sondra kicked at the dirt on the barn floor.

"No," Julius shook his head again. "You know when I was in the army I went to Mafdner on my first weekend pass. I was hoping to find it or some information about the Kleins and I found your mother instead."

Sondra nodded. She thought the story of how her parents met as romantic as any fairy tale or movie. "Did you ask Mommy about the Kleins?"

"Yes," Julius sighed and returned to his milking. "Mr. Klein had had a heart attack a few days before they were supposed to leave the country. Mommy did not know anything more."

"Did you try to find them after the war?"

"Adolf Klein is a very common name. Your Oma wrote to a number of people, but she never found anything out."

"Oh." Sondra made no attempt to hide her disappointment.

Howie was just as disappointed as she was when she reported back to him the next day, but they did not dwell much on their disappointment. There was a summer to enjoy and a bar mitzvah to get ready for.

Chapter Four

The crowd in the university chapel overflowed into the foyer. Almost all the relatives and a number of non-Jewish friends had come for Howie's bar mitzvah. The Torah reading was over and Howie made his way to the podium by himself. Sondra's palms turned sweaty and she wondered if anyone else could hear her heart beating. Only she and the visiting rabbi knew what Howie planned to say.

"My dear parents, grandparents, rabbi, friends, and relatives, as I read from the Torah, I could not help but think of my cousin, Kurt, and his special relationship with this particular Torah. This Torah scroll was used for many years in Mafdner, Germany, where my father's family had lived for generations. But in 1938 the buildup of outrage against German Jews burst into flames after a Jewish youth shot a Nazi official. This started terrible looting of Jewish homes and stores and the burning of synagogues."

Howie continued with the story of the Kristallnacht in Mafdner and Kurt's rescue of the two Torah scrolls. At the end of the story he took a deep breath.

"My cousin Kurt never had his bar mitzvah. He never made it out of Germany. I am fortunate to live in a land of freedom and to have good parents who have shown me how important it is to keep the words of the Torah alive. My father does this every day as he deals with other cattlemen honestly and my mother does this when she volunteers her time at the hospital. As a bar mitzvah I plan to do everything I can to make sure that Kurt did not save this Torah scroll in vain."

There was a hushed silence as Howie said "Amen." Sondra unclenched her hands and glanced to the side of her. She was gratified to see many of the congregants pressing handkerchiefs to their eyes and she smiled serenely at Howie. There was no doubt his speech was a success.

Sitting in front of Sondra, Irene's heart was bursting with pride. The glance she gave her parents sitting on her left seemed to say, "'I told you so.'" It was her father who had brought Herbert into her life. Meeting him in shul one morning, fifteen years ago Karl Kramer invited the personable young man for dinner and regretted it for years afterwards. He and his wife, Martha, had no objections to Herbert Apfelbaum as a man, they just did not like where he lived.

"How can you raise your kids to be Jewish in that little hick town?" Martha had ranted before the couple was even engaged.

"You know, Omaha is a great place for a cattleman," Karl had hinted once they were.

In truth, Irene would have loved for Herbert to move his ranch to Nebraska. She loved her family and the community, but she loved Herbert more, and he felt he had a moral commitment to his Uncle Simon to stay in Lincoln.

Things had not turned out so badly. Her son was an all-American boy, popular in school, good in sports, and still able to read from the Torah as well as any rabbi. Her parents smiled back at her and nodded their heads. Their hearts, too, were bursting with pride.

After the service Herbert thanked everyone for coming and invited all of them to the Holiday Inn for a luncheon. Irene was a charming hostess to all, but somehow she could not help comparing the celebration meal to the simple kosher spread her parents had made after her brother's bar mitzvah. But that had been years ago and this was the second half of the twentieth century. No one was so strictly kosher anymore that they would not eat any of the dairy foods that were being served.

On Saturday night there was a catered family dinner at Uncle Simon's house. On Sunday morning, the newspaper had quite an article about the bar mitzvah and Howie's speech. On Monday morning it was hard for Sondra to return to normalcy and go back to school.

Fortunately, her first class was World History, and Mr. Mane was her favorite teacher. Both Howie and Jane were in the same class with her. Mr. Mane began his lesson with congratulations to Howie and a brief synopsis of the Sunday article. He told his students that in a few months, when they began their unit on World War II, they would be covering the Holocaust in depth. Right before the bell rang, he called Sondra to his desk.

"Do you think your mother would be willing to talk to our class about her experiences in the work camps?"

Sondra gave her teacher a puzzled look.

"Didn't your mother tell you that we took some classes together?"

Sondra shook her head. It made sense – this *was* Mr. Mane's first year of teaching and he *had* graduated from Lincoln State. The only courses Helga took now were history courses. But Sondra's mother knew who her history teacher was. Why hadn't Helga said anything?

"Sir, my mother does not like to talk about her experiences," Sondra shook her head.

"Really?" Mr. Mane raised his eyebrows. "She shared some fascinating stories with us in class last year."

"I… I guess you can ask her," Sondra stammered, wondering if they were talking about the same person.

Mr. Mane called the following week. Sondra and her mother were cleaning up from supper when the phone rang. Sondra answered and, although she recognized her teacher's voice, she did not say anything as she handed the phone to her mother. Helga spoke softly and Sondra could not manage to hear her mother's side of the conversation. Looking pale, Helga hung up the phone and, without a word, went to her bedroom, leaving Sondra to finish the dishes.

It was in January that they began to learn about World War II and, true to his word, Mr. Mane devoted a week to the Holocaust. He began the week with a short documentary that showed American GIs liberating a concentration camp. The movie ran for thirty-seven minutes and every minute was pure torture for Sondra. Nothing in the movie was new to her, but she felt her heart beating rapidly and her face turning red, and she wondered whether everyone was looking at her. They were not. Some of the kids stared at the screen in shock, a few put their heads down on their desks, and several had tears running down their cheeks. Sondra felt Jane's comforting hand on her shoulder when the lights came on, but it was to Howie she turned for understanding. They shared a sympathetic look and as soon as the bell rang met outside in the hall.

"You okay?" Howie asked his little cousin.

Sondra nodded. "I've seen it all in books. It was just kind of uncomfortable being around all these guys, who barely ever heard of the Holocaust."

"I know." Howie was being extremely compassionate.

Mr. Mane spent the rest of the week teaching his class about the rise of the Third Reich, the various concentration and work camps, statistics of slaughter from all the Nazi-occupied countries in Europe, and excerpts from a few Holocaust-era journals. On Friday, he asked Howie to relate Oscar's story from Kristallnacht. Howie told it as well as he had done at his bar mitzvah, and Sondra was just as proud of him as she was then.

They met in the cafeteria later during lunch hour and Howie played with his milk straw and put off eating any food.

"What's on your mind?" Sondra finally asked over the din of the lunchroom.

"I've been thinking about that money Oscar gave me..."

"Yeah?" Sondra prodded.

"Maybe I don't need a car." Howie stuck his straw into his milk and took a swallow. "Maybe I should use the money to go to Germany to look for the other Torah."

Sondra opened her eyes wide. "Do you think your parents will let you?" As permissive as Uncle Herbert and Aunt Irene were, they had their limits.

"I'm not talking about going now, silly. After I finish high school, the summer before I start college."

Sondra nodded her head thoughtfully. "That will give us time to do all the research we want."

"What do you mean 'we'?"

"Don't you want me to go with you?"

"Sure," Howie exclaimed. "That would be great! Do you think *your* parents will let *you*?"

"I have four years to get them used to the idea." Sondra's left dimple deepened as she smiled.

But before they could make any more plans, two of Howie's team members hailed him and sat down at their table. Sondra was excluded from the conversation. It did not interest her anyway. She finished her food quickly and left to find Jane. However, for the next month, her main topic of conversation with Howie was how they could track down the Torah.

Chapter Five

*S*now was threatening to fall when Sondra walked up the driveway to the farmhouse. She was pleased to see Aunt Irene's car parked in front. Now she could show off the A she had gotten on her term paper to both her mother and her aunt. The two were seated at the kitchen table and so deep in conversation that they did not even hear Sondra open the door.

"Nathan has only himself to blame, if you ask me," Irene said firmly.

"I don't know," Helga sighed. "It happens a lot lately."

Sondra cleared her throat and the two women looked up, startled.

"What's wrong?"

Helga looked down at her coffee cup and Irene answered.

"Your cousin, Brenda, just got engaged to a non-Jew."

"Maybe he'll convert," Sondra offered.

"I doubt it," Irene snapped. "His grandfather is a minister."

Sondra could tell they would not be interested in her term paper. She poured herself some milk, grabbed a handful of peanuts and headed upstairs to her bedroom. As soon as she heard the engine of Irene's car start up, she headed back downstairs. Her mother was still at the kitchen table staring out of the window.

"Why does Aunt Irene blame Uncle Nathan?" Sondra asked as she settled herself across from her mother.

"She's still annoyed with him for not coming to Howie's bar mitzvah," Helga answered.

"When is the wedding?"

"In May."

"Are we going to go?"

"I don't know," Helga shook her head.

"I got an A on my history paper. Do you want to see it?"

"Of course," Helga smiled, but she seemed preoccupied and only skimmed Sondra's work.

Later, right after the store closed and while Julius was in the barn, Berta stopped by on her way home from work. As far as Sondra could remember, Berta never came by just to gossip. An efficient businesswoman who wore tailored suits and kept her gray hair cut in a short, efficient style, her two interests in life were her daughter, Bernice, and Apple's women's department. This time she spoke about neither as she settled herself in the same chair that Irene had sat in earlier.

"What do you think of Nathan's granddaughter?" Berta always came straight to the point, not caring whether Sondra was listening or not.

"It's a shame," was all Helga said.

"Sure it's a shame. But what can you expect? Once Nathan left Chicago he never made any effort to do anything Jewish with his girls. He never even went anywhere for services on the High Holidays and only once or twice he came here for Seder. Charlotte's even worse. I know she serves pork in her house. I just don't know what I'm going to tell my folks."

"I don't think Mama knows," Helga sighed. "I guess Julius or Herbert will have to tell her."

"Does Uncle Simon know?" Sondra was standing next to the sink, cutting up a salad.

Berta made a face. "There's enough bad feeling between those two brothers already. Uncle Simon may not be very religious, but he didn't rescue us from the ovens of Europe just so we could marry non-Jews."

Sondra darted a worried glance at her mother, but apparently Helga was ignoring Berta's remark about the ovens.

"I guess we'll just have to wait and see where they're going to have the ceremony," Helga said.

"And who is going to perform it," Berta retorted.

"Sure is cold out there." Julius let the kitchen door slam behind him. "Let me guess what you are so busy discussing." He grinned at the women.

"I'm sure I don't think it's funny," Berta replied hotly.

"I don't either," Julius admitted, "but I'm not going to sit down and cry about it." He put an arm around Sondra. "It's not my daughter and I hope I'll never have to face what Charlotte and her husband are facing. Right, sweetheart?"

"Right," Sondra nodded, but she felt confused. She certainly felt different that she was Jewish and she had understood for several years, ever since Bernice went off to Oklahoma University, that it was important to marry a Jew, but she wasn't sure why.

It seemed as if the phone did not stop ringing all evening. Even Aunt Lotte called from Kansas City. Frayda, Eli, and Sopha all declared that they would not go to a mixed-marriage wedding of their great-niece.

Finally, Sondra was able to get a turn at the phone. It hung on the kitchen wall in the middle of everything, but Sondra had discovered that she could pull the receiver into the bathroom, close the door, sit on the toilet seat, and have a private conversation. She called Howie, who echoed his mother's sentiments.

"But you know, since Brenda's Jewish, their kids will be Jewish," said Sondra, repeating a fact she had picked up from all her reading.

"That's fine," Howie answered, "but it's not going to help a thing if they're raised as Christians. Is your family going to go to the wedding?"

Sondra repeated what Helga had said about waiting to see where it would be.

A week later Berta had a call from Charlotte and reported

back to Helga and Irene. The wedding would be in the grandfather's church. All the relatives declared they were not going – all except Uncle Simon. Blood was thicker than water, he announced to everyone's surprise, and he was going to be at his brother's side when Nathan needed him.

For another week that was practically all the family talked about and then Friday afternoon Bernice came home for the weekend. She wasn't alone. Robert Shapiro had visited Lincoln several times with Bernice, but this time Bernice was wearing his engagement ring. Sondra squealed with delight when Bernice showed it to her. Now there was going to be a family wedding everyone could be excited about. Everyone but Uncle Simon. He was bitterly disappointed that after graduation Robert would be moving back to Philadelphia to join his father's business.

"I was counting on her taking over the children's department," he grumbled to Berta. "Mrs. Ward is retiring in a few years. What am I going to do?"

"You'll just have to find someone else," was Berta's unsympathetic reply. She knew Simon would continue to grumble up until the last minute before the wedding, but she didn't care. She also knew that he would probably give the couple their biggest wedding check.

Berta was like a woman transformed. Apple's Women's Section became just a job. Every waking hour that she wasn't at work, and quite a few when she was, was spent on wedding plans. It was not unusual at all for her to drop by Helga's or Irene's in the evenings for wedding discussions.

"Well, have they picked a date?" Helga asked a week after the announcement.

Berta nodded her head. "June 14th."

The two women were sitting in the living room. Sondra was doing her homework at the kitchen table and could not help but overhear the conversation.

"I just don't know where the wedding will be," Berta grumbled.

"Not here?" Helga was surprised.

"How can we have a kosher reception here?"

"Irene made a lovely luncheon for Howie's bar mitzvah."

"That wasn't strictly kosher and you know it," Berta frowned. "Robert's grandparents keep strictly kosher. And his aunt and uncle are so religious that they have two beds and push them apart every month."

"Your mother and father did the same," Helga remonstrated.

"That was in Germany. We're in America now!"

"Be glad, Berta," Helga spoke softly. "You could be in Charlotte's shoes."

"You're right," Berta conceded. "Robert's mother suggested that we do the wedding in Philadelphia, but I don't know. If it's there, then they'll be making the wedding and," Berta's voice became wistful, reminding Helga of the young Berta she had met when she first came to Lincoln, "I really would like to make my only child's wedding."

"Of course you would." Impulsively, Helga squeezed Berta's hand.

It was decided that the wedding would be at the chapel at Oklahoma University with the Hillel rabbi officiating. The reception would in Tulsa, half an hour's drive away, at the synagogue there.

On her next visit home, Bernice thrilled Sondra by asking her to be one of the bridesmaids. Brenda's wedding came and went with practically no one noticing it. All the family's attention was on Bernice and Robert. The wedding was less than two weeks away when Sondra came home from a dress fitting to find her mother and father sitting next to the radio. Helga was crying.

"What's the matter?" Sondra asked, more sharply than she intended.

Helga turned from the radio and bit her lip. "The Arabs attacked Israel. They're going to annihilate them."

"But America won't let that happen, right, Daddy?" Sondra turned to her father for confirmation.

Julius sat with his shoulders hunched and his eyes far away, as if he were in another room, another time. He was remembering the time he had come home from school, when he was the same age as Sondra, and found *his* mother crying next to the radio. Then she had been crying because Hitler had been made chancellor. Comforting her with the eternal optimism of youth, he had told her, "Don't worry, Hindenburg is still president." What could he say now? He had been wrong then. He sure hoped that Sondra would be right this time.

For the next few days it seemed all her parents had any enthusiasm for was to listen to the radio or watch the news on TV. It seemed as if Helga was constantly wiping her eyes and Julius was lost in thought. Sondra wondered what effect the war would have on the wedding, but was afraid to ask anyone, even Howie. Then, on Wednesday morning, everything changed. Jerusalem had been reunified. Helga was still crying, but from happiness. Two days later the war was all over.

Howie came to the farm, jubilant about Israel's victory. He reported that the tiny Jewish state was becoming the talk of the town. One rancher who his father hadn't even known was Jewish asked Herbert that morning how to buy some Israel Bonds. As Howie was bragging about Israel's triumph the phone rang. Sondra recognized her history teacher's voice and assumed that Mr. Mane wanted to speak to her mother, but he did not ask for her.

"How are you, Sondra?" he asked politely. "I'm sorry to bother you, but I was wondering who is collecting money to rebuild the Jewish Temple."

"Which one?" Sondra faltered.

"Why the one in Jerusalem, of course."

"I don't know, sir," Sondra stuttered.

"Well," Mr. Mane said, obviously disappointed, "could you find out, please? I, as well as many members of my congregation, would like to contribute."

"Yes, sir," Sondra answered politely.

She repeated the conversation to Howie, who did not understand it any better than she had.

At supper that evening, she related the dialogue to her parent's knowing looks.

"What was he talking about?"

"The Holy Temple that King Solomon built," Julius answered. "It was destroyed by the Babylonians and then rebuilt and destroyed by the Romans. That's where all the Jews used to pray and the priests used to offer their sacrifices there."

"Ooh, sacrifices." Sondra wrinkled her nose.

"Not human ones, silly," Helga laughed.

"Well, do they need money to rebuild it, or what?"

Julius shook his head. "The Arabs built a mosque where the Temple stood. If Israel were to knock that down, we would probably have a nuclear war. I'm surprised at Mr. Mane. He should know better."

"He belongs to one of those Christian groups that believe all the Jews have to be back in Israel with the Temple standing again before their savior can return," Helga explained.

"Well, what am I supposed to tell him?" Sondra demanded.

"Don't worry," Helga soothed. "I'll call him."

Bernice's wedding was four days later. It was lovely, but few of the guests spoke of how beautiful the bride was. The miracle of the victory of the tiny State of Israel was on everyone's minds, and that was almost all they talked about. Riding back to Lincoln in the same car, Howie and Sondra decided that they would add a visit to the Jewish state when they made their trip to Germany to rescue the Torah. At thirteen years old, they both believed that it would really happen.

Chapter Six

Once in ninth grade, Sondra remembered what Oscar had told her about his high school years at Lincoln High: "Everyone spoke English too fast for me to understand, and what they did speak about was all nonsense. Nothing about learning – just parties and football games." Sometimes it seemed to Sondra that classes were not important to anyone. Howie did not mind. He was on the football team and was trying out for the swim team. He also ran for student council and became one of the two representatives from the ninth grade class. Almost every Friday night there were dances or sock hops after the football games, and Howie decided they were more important than the monthly Shabbat services at the university chapel. A new fad cropped up at the high school. Boys would give their ID bracelets, with their names engraved on them, to the girls they wanted to go steady with. When Howie went out and bought one, Sondra forgot the resolution that she had made two years earlier not to criticize her cousin.

"What's that for?" Sondra asked suspiciously the first time she saw him at school with the silver bracelet around his wrist.

"I just wanted one," Howie answered with a shrug.

But later, in the lunchroom, Sondra saw him sitting with one of the ninth-grade cheerleaders and fingering his bracelet as he smiled at the girl.

"Are you going to ask Alice to go steady?" Sondra demanded

of him when they met in sixth-hour biology. The two were lab partners and could whisper together unnoticed.

"What's it to you?" Howie responded.

"She's not Jewish."

"Who here is Jewish besides you and me?"

"No one," Sondra had to admit.

"Maybe you just want to study while you're in high school, but I want to have a good time, too."

"That's really keeping the spirit of the Torah alive," Sondra muttered sarcastically.

Howie flushed angrily. "Don't worry. Maybe I'll go steady with her, but I'm not going to marry her."

"Fine, fine," Sondra suddenly remembered her resolution. "I'm sorry for sticking my nose into your business. I just know how everyone was so upset when Brenda married out."

"I'm not Brenda and I'm not going to marry out."

"Okay."

Sondra let it go, but when she returned home an hour later, Helga could see that something was troubling her daughter. She put aside her books and was ready to be a sympathetic ear.

"It's Howie," Sondra said with a sigh as she settled herself on the ledge of the kitchen window. "He's changing and doing the stupid things the other kids do."

"What stupid things?" Helga asked calmly.

Sondra described the ID bracelets, shaking her head. She wasn't sure what bothered her most; that Howie was thinking about dating a non-Jew or that he was starting to date anybody when he was only fourteen years old. In most of the childhood classics she had grown up with none of the girls ever went steady. They didn't even think about boys until they were much older. Then they usually ended up marrying the boy they had grown up with, like Peter and Heidi in the book. By rights she should marry Howie, but he was her cousin and cousins didn't get married nowadays.

"You never went steady with anybody when you were my age, did you?" Sondra demanded of her mother.

"I didn't go to school when I was your age," Helga reminded her daughter gently.

"I forgot," Sondra responded hastily. "I'm sorry."

Fortunately, Helga stayed calm. "You didn't make me stop going to school. It was a long time ago, anyway."

"Well, I think the way you and Daddy met is like a fairy tale."

"Your father certainly was like a knight in shining armor to me."

No matter how many times Sondra heard the story of her parents' romance, she never tired of it. Not that it was a story of how they met. They had known each other always, growing up in the same small village. Helga and Lotte had been best friends and Julius had never really noticed his little sister's playmate except to tease her or pull her braids. He left Mafdner when she was twelve and came back to Germany with the United States Army eight years later. He had a few days' pass and came back to see if he could find out anything about the others from the village and, of course, about the Torah. Helga had come there from the DP camps to try to discover if any of her family had survived.

Julius always described how he saw Helga from afar and would not have recognized her at all except for the defiant way she held her chin. Helga always said that she recognized him immediately. Of course, he hadn't been in the camps. Together they went to Helga's home and found that it had been stripped bare.

That evening Julius had gone to the burgermeister. Old Hans Richter, with his bald, red head that matched his bulbous red nose, had been the head of the village before the Nazis, during the time of the Nazis, and after the Nazis. He swore up and down he had only done what he had been forced to do, but Julius knew better. Wearing his army uniform, Julius had handed him a list of things Helga needed and told Richter to get them for her. According to

Julius, the burgermeister had scanned the list and looked back at Julius.

"Where am I supposed to get all these things?" he had whined.

"The people who helped you destroy the homes and synagogue can help you."

"But I have to be out in the field first thing tomorrow morning to gather in the hay."

At that point something snapped in Julius. Perhaps it was the shock of seeing the Jewish cemetery in ruins that morning. Maybe it was seeing his kid sister's best chum an orphan. Whatever the reason, Julius lost his temper. He pulled out his .45 and stuck it in the man's gut. "You have everything here by tomorrow!"

Even after hearing the story so many times, it was hard for Sondra to imagine her father so furious. Unlike Uncle Herbert, who lost his temper about once a week, Sondra could count on one hand the number of times she had seen her father angry.

Still, the mayor had been sufficiently intimidated by the Jewish soldier that he had everything on the list ready the next day. Julius made arrangements for Helga to go to America and stay with his parents. By the time he got out of the army and came home, Helga had put on weight and grown more hair, and he fell in love with her. They were married and moved into their own home. Helga had hoped to fill it with lots of children but, now, after six miscarriages over the years, she regarded Sondra as her miracle.

"Sondra," she spoke softly, "you and Howie are cousins and good friends, but you have to realize Howie has a much different personality from yours. He doesn't have your strength of character." Helga held up her hand to stem her daughter's protest. "He can't handle being different and will always want to be part of the crowd."

"I don't think that's true," Sondra spoke resentfully. She had confided in her mother, and now Helga had spoiled it with her criticisms of Howie. It seemed that lately, her mother was always saying the wrong things.

Later, when she was doing her homework, Sondra thought over the conversation with Howie. She did not want to do nothing but study for the next four years, but she was not sure what else she wanted to do. There were all sorts of school clubs she could join such as the language clubs, Future Homemakers, Future Teachers and the Chess Club, to name a few, but they all sounded boring. She was still on the newspaper staff, but that was almost like studying. Jane went to a lot of parties on the weekends with her church youth group, but that wasn't for Sondra. She thought about doing volunteer work at the hospital. However, she had a squeamish stomach. Besides, while that might be a nice thing to do, it wasn't for fun. Sondra wondered how Bernice had gotten through her high school years and agreed with Uncle Simon that it was a shame that she and Robert were living in Philadelphia.

The next day at school, Alice was wearing Howie's ID bracelet. For the ninth graders at Lincoln High, "going steady" meant that they ate lunch together, walked together from class to class, sometimes holding hands, and went to the school dances together. Most couples went steady for about a month and then "broke up." Sondra looked at Howie and Alice sitting next to each other in the lunchroom and wondered how long they would last. She was feeling more than a little resentful when Jane sat down next to her.

"I've got a great idea!"

"What?" Sondra turned gratefully to her friend, happy to have a diversion.

"Let's join the drama club."

"Can we?"

Jane nodded her head and opened her bag of chips. "I spoke to Carla Brooks and she said the freshmen can't do any acting, but that there was a lot more to a production than the actors. They need us to work back stage, paint scenery, gather props, and fix costumes. If we like it, we can take drama as one of our electives next year. What do you think?" Jane held the bag out to Sondra.

"I can't really see myself on stage," Sondra hesitated as she took a handful of Fritos, "but it sounds like it would be really fun to be backstage."

It was! Sondra loved the teamwork involved in transforming a plain wooden stage and simple high school students into a whole new reality. There were two other freshman girls who joined the club, Christine Barnes and Joy Charles. Christine was from a large farm north of town where she lived with her grandparents. Tall and blonde, she was a classic beauty, but shy. Joy had long, black hair and clear, light skin. She would have looked like Snow White, Sondra thought, if she didn't have a weight problem. Neither Christine nor Joy was into dating, and the four girls spent a lot of time hanging out together, having fun.

Between sports practice, student council, dating, and studying, Howie had little time for his cousin. Sondra watched him break up with Alice, give his ID bracelet to another girl, break up with her, and quickly find another girl to go steady with. One afternoon Sondra overheard her mother and Aunt Irene discussing Howie's girlfriends.

"It's so silly, this going steady," Aunt Irene laughed. "Where can they go? Herbert carpools Howie and his latest girlfriend to the dance and the girl's father picks up. It's ridiculous. When I was in high school, the boy borrowed his father's car to pick up the girl."

"So none of the boys dated until they were sixteen?" Helga asked.

Irene shook her head. "Only if they walked somewhere. I would have been embarrassed to have my date's father pick me up. Herbert can't stand it. Howie and the girl sit in the back seat and the girl just giggles and Howie acts self-conscious. I don't know what his hurry is anyway."

Sondra wondered why her aunt and uncle let Howie go out if

they thought it was so absurd. She didn't ask, though. She wanted to stay on good terms with Howie for the Hanukkah party.

In the spring, Mrs. Wiggs, the drama teacher, chose *The Diary of Anne Frank* for the play. Backstage rumors had it that Mrs. Wiggs had once been on Broadway and gave it all up to marry Mr. Wiggs. It was hard to believe, though. She was so heavy that her forearms shook like raw bread dough, and Sondra could not imagine her on the stage in any but the most absurd part. Still, the middle-aged woman knew the theater and understood how to get the most out of her students for a professional production.

Sondra became the unofficial expert on the Holocaust, winning the respect of the whole cast. Enthusiastic about the play, Sondra tried to talk her parents into going to see it until she discovered that the first performance would be on the same Friday night as the monthly services. Sondra did not know what to do. She had been disappointed in Howie for choosing the dances over the services, but that had been a regular thing. She would only be missing once. Everyone missed services once in a while.

"You do what you have to do," Mrs. Wiggs spoke kindly when Sondra told her about her dilemma. "We sure would like to have you here, but we can cover for you if you need."

Jane had overheard the conversation and was skeptical. "She's just saying that to be nice. She wouldn't want anyone to think she's an anti-Semite, especially if she's putting on *The Diary of Anne Frank*."

There was no use asking Howie his advice. Sondra knew he would tell her to forget the services. Her parents gave her their permission to skip one month, but Sondra still hesitated.

For as long as she could remember, Sondra had been taught that she was special because she was Jewish. She knew that she was different, but she really did not understand why. Her cousin Brenda had been different, too, but she had crossed the line. What had kept Bernice from crossing the line? What, she wondered, would keep her and Howie from marrying out? Their kosher homes? The Hanukkah parties? The Passover seder? Family ties? Perhaps it was the monthly services. Sondra was afraid if she missed one month, it would be easier to miss the next month, and who knew where it would lead?

That Sunday, Aunt Lotte and her family came in for the day and everyone gathered at Frayda's house. As usual, the men assembled in the dining room, the women in the living room, and the children were on the front porch. When Oscar arrived he spent a few minutes inside and then returned to the porch.

"How are you all doing?" He visited with the youngsters for a bit and then asked Sondra to take a walk with him. They headed out back, past the vegetable garden.

"Your Opa sure loved his garden," Oscar remarked.

"Uh-hum," Sondra agreed. "It's hard for Oma to keep up with it, but Howie, Lisa, and I try to help out."

"You do," Oscar nodded his head as he studied the garden for a while. "You are good kids," he continued. "Real good kids. Your dad was talking to me about your predicament yesterday."

"Yeah." Sondra waited for Oscar to proceed.

"Well, I think you should know that there are going to be services twice in May."

"Twice?" Sondra repeated. "Why?"

"The normal Shabbos one and a special one for Shavuos."

"Really?" Sondra brightened. "Then I can work on the play and still go to Shavuos services. Thank you, Oscar." She planted a kiss on her cousin's cheek and practically skipped as they made their way back to the house.

"Do you really think that the monthly services are that important?" Howie asked seriously after Sondra had explained her solution to him. She just nodded her head.

"Maybe," Howie responded, "I'll make more of an effort to go. I've kind of missed them."

Sondra's dimple deepened with her smile and inside she felt she could fly from happiness.

Chapter Seven

*I*f Sondra had known how much agitation her invitation to the spring play would cause Helga, she would never have suggested it. Ever since she was eleven years old, she had tried to be sensitive to her mother's past, but Sondra was still only fourteen. She had not thought *The Diary of Anne Frank* would be problematic, since it did not deal with the camps at all. For Helga, however, it was an opening to a door that she did not want to go through, at least not with her family by her side.

Helga's college courses were her way of coping with all the horrors she had suffered. Somehow, she reasoned, if she learned enough world history, she would be able to understand why it had happened. Her dream was, in time, to get her doctorate and funding to begin a Holocaust Studies Department at Lincoln State. She was able to relate some of her worst experiences in the college classroom, but with her own family she was mute. Julius was understanding and his family was accepting, but Helga worried about how long Sondra would be patient with her mother's silence on the subject.

When Sondra had entered junior high school, Helga had worried about how her daughter would do socially. Her two best friends from grammar school had moved during the summer, and Helga did not want Sondra leaning on Howie. With trepidation, she watched her daughter's growing friendship with the Methodist minister's daughter.

Sondra was too young to remember how Bernice had wanted to join the youth group at the Baptist church just so she would have someplace to socialize. Berta had had her hands full with that. Everyone had understood Bernice's need, but they all agreed that Berta had been right to forbid it. Fortunately for all, Professor Cohen had come to the university and his daughter and Bernice became good friends.

As far as Helga could see, Jane didn't proselytize. Her suggestion that she and Sondra get involved with the drama department had been excellent for Sondra. Now she had a group of friends and a busy social life. Helga hoped it would keep her satisfied until she graduated from high school. She decided she must do her best to encourage Sondra and so she agreed to go to the show. Afterwards, Helga told her daughter that it had been an excellent production, especially for a high school, but that was all she would say about the topic.

Sondra swallowed her disappointment that the play had not opened up a discussion with her mother and concentrated on final exams. Once summer came, she was really busy. There were cookouts at Christine's farm, boat rides on the river in Joy's family's rowboat, and sleepovers at Jane's. Julius took all the girls to the rodeo and the county fair, where Frayda won first prize for her embroidery. Joy suggested that they volunteer at Head Start, and the girls spent several hours a week working with Afro-American pre-schoolers. Uncle Simon asked Howie and Sondra to help out at the store during the three-day sidewalk sale, which was a lot of fun. There were plays at the university summer theater and a new movie each week at the Orpheum. Still, when vacation ended, Sondra was happy to go back to school. She had signed up for Drama I and it was her first class every morning, a great way to start the day.

They had been in school a month when Mrs. Wiggs announced that the yearly musical would be *The King and I*. Only music students would be allowed to try out for the main parts, but there were parts for the tone-deaf drama students, too. Jane, Christine, and Joy all urged Sondra to try out for one of the children's parts. Being so petite, and with black hair and dark eyes, she would be perfect, they declared. After hearing their encouragement for a week, Sondra went to the tryouts with her heart beating wildly. Two days later the cast list was posted: Sondra was one of the children and so was Jane. Mrs. Wiggs had told Jane that her blonde hair would not be a problem. There were wigs and hair rinses to change the color of hair, but, Mrs. Wiggs declared, she had no solution to making a high school student smaller.

Learning lines, costume fittings, and play practice took up almost all of Sondra's time and thoughts. A willing worker, she radiated enthusiasm and team spirit and caught the eye of Roger Morris, the junior who played the King of Siam. It was a wonderful two months and then came the final performance, the cast party, and it was all over. Before Sondra could get depressed, though, Roger asked her to go with him to the winter prom. She had totally forgotten about her indignation with Howie for giving his ID bracelet to non-Jewish girls. She also felt that at the age of fifteen she was old enough to start dating, especially if the boy was already sixteen. Despite the stormy day outside, Sondra's face was full of sunshine when she came home with her good news.

"Mom, guess what!" she called as she wiped her feet.

"What?" Helga stuck her pencil behind her ear as she rose from her studies to greet her daughter.

"Roger Morris asked me to the winter prom!"

"Roger?" Helga asked, preoccupied. "He's the one who was in the play with you?"

"No," Sondra laughed. "I was in the play with him."

"He brought you home from practice a few times?"

"Almost always." Sondra nodded, wondering why her mother was not showing more enthusiasm.

"Is he friends with Howie at all?" Helga was grabbing at these seemingly inane questions as she tried to decide, on her own, without talking to Julius, how to tell Sondra she could not go out with this non-Jew.

"They're friendly, yeah," Sondra shrugged, walked into the kitchen, and opened the refrigerator.

"What does his father do?" Helga followed her daughter.

"He's a lawyer," Sondra tried to keep the impatience out of her voice.

"Oh, he has an office downtown."

"I guess so. What are all these questions for?" Sondra's voice rose and she bit her lip to control it. "Why can't you just be happy for me? Why am I getting the third degree? Other mothers would be thrilled to have their daughters asked out by one of the nicest, most popular boys in the school."

"I'm not like other mothers," Helga spoke softly. Her tone was dangerous. Sondra knew in a minute her mother would go into one of her icy silences.

Sondra took a deep breath and spoke softly, too. "I know, Mom. You're great as you are. I just want you to be happy for me."

"I know," Helga smiled sadly, "but Roger isn't Jewish." It was said as innocuously as if Roger did not have curly hair. Still, Sondra caught the message and tears welled up in her eyes. Before anything more could be said she ran upstairs and threw herself across her bed and began crying.

She cried for herself. Why did she always have to be different from everyone else? Why could Howie do things that she couldn't? Why couldn't they live in a place where there were more Jews? Why couldn't her mother understand her better? It was that thought that made Sondra catch her breath. Turning over on her back, she studied the crack in the ceiling and concentrated on her mother. Poor Helga. Of course she couldn't understand. Her high school years had been spent in a work camp and she had never gone to any dances with anyone, Jewish or not. She had no idea how it would feel the next couple of weeks to listen to all the other girls talking about their new dresses and what kind of corsages they wanted. Even Jane was going. She had been asked to the dance already a week ago. Probably Christine would be asked, too. Sondra had noticed that the quiet senior, who had played the prime minister, was interested in her friend. At least Joy would, most likely, not be asked. Sondra supposed the two of them could go to the movies on the night of the prom. They certainly would have no trouble finding a good seat. No one else would be there.

Blinking hard to keep the tears from falling again, Sondra looked around her room and studied it as if she was seeing it for the first time. The white, muslin curtains at the windows, the pink and gold-stripped wallpaper that matched the bedspreads on the twin beds could be found in hundreds of teenagers' rooms across America. The gold and white furniture that she and her mother had traveled together to Augusta to buy was beautiful, but dozens of girls in Lincoln had similar such furniture. What was it that made Sondra feel so different? As always, whenever she pondered the question, she vividly remembered that day, four years earlier, when she first learned of the tragedy her mother had suffered.

Other girls she knew would have screamed at their mothers if they had tried to keep them from going to the prom. Or they would have pouted until their mothers gave in. Or appealed to their fathers, or grandparents, or someone to be on their side. Sondra knew she would do none of those things. Ever since she was eleven years old, she had felt a need to protect her mother as much as she could. In the past year she had talked to Jane and the others enough to know that all the irritations she felt with Helga were a normal part of adolescence. Still, she wondered whether Helga knew that they were normal.

Life seemed unfair. She was finally beginning to feel like a normal teenager with a real boyfriend. Hanging out on the weekends with just Jane, Christine, and Joy no longer seemed like so much fun. Aunt Irene's Hanukkah party did not sound exciting either. Nothing sounded exciting. Sondra did not want to go downstairs for dinner, she did not want to go to school the following day, and she certainly did not want to face Roger and explain to him that she would not be able to go to the dance with him. She felt as if she could see a little devil from her old comic books at her shoulder telling her to stay in bed and hide from the world for as long as she wanted. At the same time, though, there was an obnoxious little angel at her other shoulder telling her to pull herself together.

Just as it seemed that the little angel was winning, the phone rang.

"Sondra," Helga called from the foot of the stairs, "it's for you."

Reluctantly, hoping that it wasn't Roger, she picked up the pink Princess phone that had been her birthday present and heard her Aunt Lotte's voice.

"How are you doing, dear?"

"Okay," Sondra tried to make her voice sound cheerful.

"We were wondering if you could help us out here?"

"How?"

"In a few weeks, Joey is going to have a special part in Shabbos morning services and you know how he looks up to you."

"Oh?"

"Well, he wants to know if you can come here to watch him."

"When?"

It was no surprise that Aunt Lotte mentioned the same date as the dance. Sondra was certain her mother had orchestrated the invitation and she was sure Aunt Lotte knew that she knew. Still, she didn't care. It would give her an excuse to get out of town and away from everything. As far as she was concerned, she'd be happy to go right then.

Sondra confided in Howie the next day at school. He was in between girlfriends and the two sat together in the lunchroom. To Howie's credit, he did not even hint that Sondra had criticized him only a year earlier for going out with a non-Jew. He just listened and was all sympathy.

"I just don't know what to say to Roger," Sondra concluded, playing with her roll instead of eating it.

"Would you like me to explain to him about your parents?"

"Would you?" Sondra smiled gratefully.

That afternoon at sport practice her cousin pulled Roger aside and explained why Sondra would not be able to go to the dance with him and how badly she felt. Roger called that evening to tell Sondra he understood.

"We can still be friends, can't we?" he asked.

"Of course," Sondra answered happily. But, she heard through the school grapevine that Roger had asked another girl to the dance the following week. Sondra knew that there would be no more long talks together or rides home. While the other girls were buying their prom dresses, Sondra went shopping with Helga to buy a new outfit for Kansas City. And while many of the girls got out of school early on the Friday of the prom so they could go to the hairdresser, Sondra did not go at all. Instead, she boarded the Greyhound bus that would take her to Kansas City.

Chapter Eight

The sanctuary of the Ohev Shalom synagogue was at least four times the size of the little chapel at Lincoln State. There were three sections of seats – one on the right for men, another on the left for the women, and a third for mixed seating. Sondra and the Katzners sat in the middle section. The services were much longer than the services at home and everything was in Hebrew. In the middle of the *haftarah*, the reading from the Prophets, Sondra gave up trying to follow and began studying her surroundings.

Across the aisle, in the women's section sat a blonde girl, about Sondra's age. She was wearing a powder-blue turtleneck sweater and she had a silver charm bracelet on her wrist that jingled every time she turned the page. Her shoulder-length hair was brushed in the classic flip that all the teenage girls who had manageable hair wore. No matter what Sondra did, her flip lasted only an hour, at the most, each morning and then hung down straight for the rest of the day.

"Who is that?" She whispered to Rachel.

"Debbie Greenbaum, the cantor's daughter."

Aunt Lotte shushed the two of them with a frown, but later, after Joey had sung the Song of Praise at the end of the service, Rachel introduced the two girls and then walked away to join her friends. Debbie and Sondra entered the social hall together, listened to Kiddush, the special Shabbat blessing over the wine, filled their plates, and sat down together.

Debbie, who was taller than Sondra, was a quite pretty girl with dreamy green eyes and metal braces on her teeth. She moved with poise and seemed full of self-confidence.

"What grade are you in?" Debbie asked, once she learned that Sondra was Rachel's cousin from Lincoln.

"I'm a sophomore. What about you?"

"The same. Have you started thinking about colleges yet?"

"Not really," Sondra shrugged. "I know I'll be going out of state, though. Do you know where you want to go?"

"I'll probably go to Stern College."

"Where's that?"

"New York."

Sondra's eyes grew big. "That's a long way from home!"

Debbie nodded. "That's the drawback."

Before Sondra could think of anything to say, they were joined by a teenage boy with a plate piled with gefilte fish balls, herring, and cake.

"Marc," Debbie made the introductions. "This is Sondra. She's visiting the Katzners."

"Good Shabbos," Marc smiled. He pushed his wire-framed glasses back up on his nose where they belonged and began attacking his food.

"Did Debbie tell you about our ice-skating party tonight?"

"Give me a chance," Debbie laughed. "Our youth group will be having a party tonight. Would you like to come?"

"That would be nice," Sondra's eyes sparkled at the idea. "If my aunt will let me."

"She will. I'll call you tonight, motza'ei Shabbos, when Shabbos is over."

Just then Uncle Manny motioned that they were leaving.

"My father is ready, too," Debbie announced. "I'll walk out with you."

They both said goodbye to Marc. When they got outside,

though, Debbie and her father did not go to the parking lot as the Katzners did. Instead they left the shul grounds walking.

"They don't drive on Shabbat?" Sondra asked once she was inside her cousins' station wagon.

"Of course not," Aunt Lotte answered. "He's our cantor. He's shomer Shabbos, he has to keep Shabbos."

"Oh." Sondra nodded. She knew her parents had kept Shabbat in Germany, but she didn't know anyone in America who did.

"Did you like shul?" Joey asked.

"Yeah," Sondra hesitated. "It was longer than I was used to, but you sang very nicely."

Joey beamed at the compliment.

After lunch Sondra played a marathon game of Monopoly with her cousins. They stopped only when Rachel had a phone call from a school friend asking her to go bowling. Once she left, Joey turned on the T V. There was a show about fishing that did not interest Sondra at all, so she went to her room and curled up with a book. She must have fallen asleep because the next thing she knew her aunt was knocking on the door.

"You have a phone call, Sondra."

Lotte was happy to give permission for her niece to go to the skating party.

"We'll pick you up at eight," Debbie instructed. "Be ready."

At eight o'clock a horn honked in front of the house. Rachel looked out the front window and announced that Brian Cohen was the driver. Sondra said her good-byes and raced out to the yellow Mustang that idled in the driveway. Debbie was already in the back and Sondra squeezed in next to her. She was introduced to the Goldstein twins and to Brian. Marc, Brian's brother, was sitting in the passenger seat. As they got out of the car at the skating rink, both Marc and Brian reached into their pockets to pull out skullcaps and set them on their heads. It was the first time Sondra had ever seen anyone with a yarmulke outside home or shul. She was surprised they weren't self-conscious.

The lights were bright inside the crowded rink and Sondra

easily spotted eight more boys with yarmulkes. With them were a dozen more girls and they were all gathered around a middle-aged man with a black hat and beard. Debbie introduced him as Mr. Marcus, the youth group director.

Since there were no skating rinks in Lincoln, it was Sondra's first time skating. Gliding across the frozen pond in her boots was not the same thing at all She lost count of how many times she fell down during the first fifteen minutes, but Marc and Debbie always came to her rescue. Each of them took one of her hands and taught her the ropes. In no time, she was skating in rhythm to the Beach Boys tunes blaring over the loud speaker. By the time The Mamas and the Papas record was on, though, she needed to stop and catch her breath. She joined Mr. Marcus at the little table he sat at next to the rink. Scattered across the table were bottles of soft drinks and a stack of Dixie cups. He motioned for her to help herself and Sondra took some 7-UP.

"Kansas City must be a lot different from Lincoln," Mr. Marcus commented as Sondra swallowed her first sip.

Forty years old, with more than a few gray hairs and a middle-aged paunch, Mr. Marcus seemed a most unlikely youth group director. Yet there was something in his manner that made him easy to talk to. In just a few minutes Sondra was describing some of her problems growing up Jewish, problems that she had never even discussed with Howie.

She had just finished confiding how much she hated the December holiday season at school when Debbie left the rink. Fanning herself with her hand she came to their table.

"Can I join you, or are you having a private conversation?"

"No," Sondra grinned. "Sit down."

"You know, Debbie," Mr. Marcus said, "Sondra and I were discussing how difficult it is for her to have almost no other Jewish students in her high school."

"I know," Debbie nodded. "In my biology class there is just one other Jewish girl. She did not take off for Sukkos, and I don't think the teacher really believed that I was missing school for religious reasons. She seems to have had it in for me ever since then."

Debbie paused to pour herself some Dr. Pepper.

"Debbie," Mr. Marcus said, "do you realize that in Sondra's whole school there are only two Jews? Forget about how many are in her classes."

"Oh," Debbie put her hand over her mouth in embarrassment, "I guess everything is relative."

Just then Anna Goldstein fell on the ice and cut her knee. Mr. Marcus left the two girls and went to take care of Anna. It didn't take long before Sondra found herself confiding in Debbie everything about Roger and the prom.

"My parents don't let me date either," Debbie told Sondra. "Not even Jewish boys, but I have a lot of fun with all the activities Mr. Marcus organizes for us. Maybe you can come for some of them."

"Maybe," Sondra smiled at the idea. She wondered if her parents would allow it.

"Okay, boys and girls, it's time to choose partners!" The record had stopped and the manager was now using the loud speaker. "We're going to square dance on the ice!"

"Come on, Debbie!" Marc called. "You're my partner."

Sondra watched her friend take Marc's hand. "She may not be able to date," Sondra thought, "but I bet Marc considers her his girlfriend." She settled herself down ready to watch the others, when there was a tap on her shoulder. Brian was standing behind her.

"Be my partner?"

"Sure!"

Aunt Lotte was up waiting for her when she came home.

"Did you have a good time, dear?"

Sondra smiled at her sweet-faced aunt who looked so much like the old pictures of her grandmother. "I had a great time. No one treated me like I was a stranger or different. I felt like I really belonged."

"I'm glad," Lotte replied. As she watched her niece leave the room, she resolved to invite Sondra often. Like Irene, she thought that her brother should move his family to Kansas City, but not so much for Helga's sake as for Sondra's. There was something unique about her niece that made it hard for Sondra to fit into an all-American crowd. It had not really been a problem for Bernice or Howie and most likely would not be a problem for Lisa. Perhaps the fact that Helga was a survivor was what made Sondra different. Well, Lotte thought, her mother would be coming this year for the Passover Seders. Maybe Sondra could come with her.

Chapter Nine

*L*otte waited until close to Passover to approach Helga with her idea, and when she did, she did it via letter so that she could sound casual.

"Instead of Julius or Herbert bringing Mama up," she wrote, "why don't you send her on the bus with Sondra as a chaperone?"

The letter continued with all sorts of family news that did little to cheer Helga. Lotte's suggestion had thrown her into emotional turmoil. Sondra had had such a wonderful visit to Kansas City and Helga knew her daughter was anxious to go back. But not to have her at their own Seder? Sooner or later that was going to happen. Bernice certainly had not come back from Philadelphia for Passover once she was married. But Sondra was only fifteen. To even think about her not being at their Seder was unbearable. Perhaps they should all go to Kansas City? But who would milk the cows? Helga was nervous and distracted when Sondra burst into the house after school with the news that she had a part in the spring play.

"That's wonderful, dear," Helga said absently. "What's your part?"

"I'll tell you about it at dinner." Sondra headed upstairs, refusing to let her mother's lack of enthusiasm dampen hers. She had been given the part of Betty Parris in Arthur Miller's *The Crucible*. Although it was barely a speaking part and another child's part also, Mrs. Wiggs had pulled her aside before class to speak to her.

"I don't want you to think that you just got that part because you're the smallest girl in the drama department," the drama teacher said, shaking her finger at Sondra and making her forearm shake. "There were a couple of other girls we could have made do with, but it's a challenging part and I think you can do it."

"Thank you." Sondra's eyes shone at her teacher's praise.

"And another thing," Mrs. Wiggs said, putting her hand on Sondra's shoulder. "I think you should sign up for music next year. There's no reason that you should not have a good part in our musical."

"Okay," Sondra stammered. She wasn't sure how she would fit music into her schedule, but she'd find a way.

Jane's and Joy's names were on the cast list, too. They had non-speaking parts as two of the town girls. Christine was co-chairperson of the costume committee. Before coming home, the four girls had met at Molly's Drugstore for a soda and to celebrate. Sondra wondered if her friends had met with more enthusiasm at their homes than she had.

She was lost in her script when her father came home. Helga met him at the door and thrust Lotte's letter at him. She handed him a cup of coffee as he read.

"Ridiculous," he announced tossing the letter in the trash. "Sondra's place is with us. Besides, Herbert and I already worked it out. He's taking Mama down erev Pesah and I'll pick her up Sunday. Wait a minute," Julius smiled at his wife. "There's no reason why Sondra can't come with me Sunday to get Mama. For that matter, you can come, too. We can make a day of it."

Helga shared Julius's enthusiasm. By the time Sondra came down for supper the plans were set and her parents were eager to hear all about the play. Sondra never knew about her aunt's original suggestion, but she probably would not have been willing to miss so many days of practice, anyway. Later, when she found out that Mr. Marcus had a boating party planned for the youth group the Sunday afternoon during Passover, she was ecstatic.

"I really want to go," she told her father. "Can we stay in Kansas City until the party's over?" she begged.

Julius agreed. It would mean he wouldn't be back in time to milk the cows and he'd have to pay someone to come in and do it, but the sparkle in Sondra's eyes made it worthwhile.

They left Lincoln early, as soon as the milking and breakfast dishes were out of the way, and already had a nice visit and lunch when Debbie knocked at the door.

"I hope it's okay that I came early."

"Sure." Uncle Manny invited the cantor's daughter into the dining room and made introductions. The meal was finished. Heavy from *matza*, everyone was still seated around the table.

"How about joining us for dessert?" Lotte asked.

"Okay," Debbie smiled.

"We'll clear, Aunt Lotte," Sondra had already risen.

"The guest should not clear," Frayda remonstrated.

Sondra just laughed. "Oma, it will give us a chance to talk."

"Do you want me to help?" Rachel asked politely and was relieved when Sondra shook her head.

"Your grandmother is really cute," Debbie said as she scraped a plate into the trash.

"I know," Sondra smiled. "She's special. She's the only grandparent I have left."

"I don't have any."

"No?" Sondra's head was in the refrigerator looking for a place for the leftover salad.

"All of mine were killed in the camps," Debbie confided.

Sondra stood up, salad still in her hand. "They were?" she whispered. "So were mine, at least my mother's parents. Were your parents in the camps, too?"

"My mother was." Debbie turned from the trash and also

lowered her voice. "My father was a partisan. What about your parents?"

"My father was here, but my mother was in a work camp. She doesn't talk about it."

"My mother doesn't like to talk about it either."

"You know," Sondra said, "you're the only person I know, except for me, whose mother came out of the camps. Maybe that's why I feel so comfortable with you."

"I know," Debbie nodded. "Do you want to write letters back and forth?"

"I'd love to!"

Sondra did not find it as easy to write Debbie as she thought it would be. Her friend had never been in Lincoln or met anyone from there. Sondra felt she was always getting bogged down in explanations of people and places. Debbie's letters, on the other hand, were full of news of the kids from the youth group and Sondra eagerly waited for the blue-flowered envelopes with Debbie's curly script. Coming home from a particularly trying play practice, she was pleased to see one of Debbie's letters propped up next to the flower vase on the kitchen table.

> Dear Sondra,
>
> Hope all is well with you. It seems like Pesah was ages ago instead of just last week. I'm still enjoying the bread, though. How about you?
>
> I have a ton of homework to make up for all the school I missed. Anna fell and broke her arm playing volleyball last week. Poor thing. She'll be in a cast when the pool opens. I can't wait for it to open. It's so *hot* here and it's not even May!
>
> Guess what! May 9th and 10th we're having a mini-Shabbaton here. We're doing it with a shul from St. Louis. Everyone will sleep in houses near the shul and we'll eat all our meals there. Saturday night we'll have a big bonfire and

cookout. Mr. Marcus said I could invite you. Please come. You can stay with me. Write back soon and let me know you are coming. It will be a lot of fun!

    Bye,

       Debbie

Sondra finished reading the letter and slowly laid it back on the kitchen table. The Shabbaton probably would be a lot of fun. Why couldn't it be a week later? Why did it have to be the same weekend as the play? With a sigh Sondra took out her stationery and wrote a quick reply, writing all about the play and explaining why she would not be able to come for the Shabbaton.

"But," she wrote at the end and hoped it did not sound too forward, "maybe I can come for a weekend after the play is over."

Sealing the envelope, she found a stamp and walked out to the road to place it in the mailbox. As she lifted the little red flag to alert the postman to the enclosed letter, she resolved to forget about the Shabbaton and to do her best for the play.

The Crucible was quite a serious undertaking for a high school production. A tragedy, it told the story of how the Salem witch hunt, run by men who thought they were justified, destroyed the lives of a number of decent families. Cast members could easily be picked out in the cafeteria by the serious conversations they were having.

"I understand why Proctor refused to indict any of the others," Joy set her tray on the lunchroom table.

"I guess so," Christine sat down. "But those people were going to die anyway. He could have saved his life."

"They were going to accept his confession," Jane put her lunch change into her purse, "without him naming any names. But he didn't want his confession hanging on the church door."

"If I had been there," Sondra nibbled on a piece of cheese, "I would have confessed at the very beginning and taken my family and run away to Virginia or someplace."

"You wouldn't have been there," Jane said dryly. "They were all Puritan Christians and would not have tolerated a Jew."

Joy laughed uncomfortably and Sondra felt her face redden.

"After all the persecution they suffered in England," Christine's quiet voice broke the silence, "it's amazing how intolerant the Puritans were."

"Their lives seemed so grim," Joy added.

"Just look at all the costumes," Christine said. "Black, gray, and dark blue."

"Not very colorful," Jane agreed. "But the way they talked is so neat."

"That's about the only thing that was neat."

"Don't forget, they were all deeply religious people. They all believed in God."

Sondra wondered if her friends noticed how silent she had become. If the people of Salem were religious, then she wanted to stay far away from religious people. For the first time in their friendship, Jane had made Sondra feel uncomfortable because she was Jewish. Sondra resolved to stop discussing *The Crucible* and just worry about her part.

Roger had been given the part of Reverend Parris, Betty's father and they needed to interact on the stage. At first, Sondra had been uncomfortable being so close to one of the most popular boys in the school, who had asked her to the prom. Roger was diplomatic, though. He was able to be friendly and at the same time make sure that Sondra knew that he was now going steady with Mindy Hansen, who played Elizabeth Proctor. All of them took their parts seriously and, in the end, Mrs. Wiggs had an excellent production of *The Crucible*.

Chapter Ten

*T*hree weeks later, when Sondra boarded the Greyhound bus for Kansas City, she left Lincoln full of self-confidence and pride at a job well done. Aunt Lotte would again be at the bus station to meet her, but this time Sondra was going to stay at Debbie's house. In the beginning Helga had not liked the idea of Sondra staying with strangers. Lotte had called her childhood friend, though, and convinced her that the Greenbaum family was a good family and that it would be a lot more fun for Sondra to stay there.

"Not that we don't love having Sondra stay with us," Lotte had explained. "She is welcome whenever she wants, but Debbie is a lovely girl and a good friend for Sondra. She needs a Jewish friend."

Sondra spent the afternoon with her cousins and then, an hour before Shabbat Aunt Lotte drove her the half a mile to Debbie's home. The house was a simple three-bedroom, white frame house, painfully neat with rows and rows of bookcases filled with books in five different languages. Debbie introduced Sondra to her parents and Sondra was surprised to hear their strong East European accents. She even had a little trouble understanding what Debbie's mother said and gave Debbie a questioning look.

"My mother wants you to take out your non-Shabbos items before she lights candles."

"Oh?" Sondra still did not understand.

"You know, like money or pencils or a nail kit. Things that you're not allowed to use on Shabbos. Put them in a special place so you won't touch them."

"Okay," Sondra nodded, suddenly feeling shy and uncomfortable.

"Come on," Debbie took Sondra's bag, "I'll show you to my room."

Debbie's room was a contrast to the neatness of the rest of the house. Her lilac wallpaper was plastered with photographs and souvenirs. The desk was stacked high with books and papers. And the guest bed was covered with stuffed animals.

"This is your bed," Debbie pushed the animals underneath. "You can put your *muktza* things in this drawer."

"My what?"

"Muktza," Debbie repeated. "You know, the things you're not supposed to touch on Shabbos."

"I've never kept Shabbos," Sondra hesitated, wondering if maybe she should call Aunt Lotte to come pick her up. "What if I make a mistake?"

"Don't worry," Debbie understood her friend's discomfort. "It's not that difficult. There will be tape on the light switches to remind you not to turn them on and off. We'll take the phone off the hook and, of course, you know not to turn on the TV or radio, right?"

Sondra nodded.

"In the bathroom there's torn toilet paper and my mother and I will take care of things in the kitchen, and you know we're going to walk to shul tomorrow, okay?"

"Okay," Sondra took a deep breath.

"And if you make a mistake," Debbie laughed, "no one is going to stone you."

That reminded Sondra of the Puritans of Salem and as she unpacked she explained *The Crucible* to Debbie. She told her about the lunchroom discussion with her friends and how she found it so hard to understand how the Puritans thought.

"The whole witch hunt trials were based on lies. Those people knew they weren't witches. What did it matter if they said they were and then ran away to start a new life?"

"It's hard to understand them," Debbie said thoughtfully, "because their religion is so different from ours."

"I always thought they were so similar," Sondra objected. "We're always hearing about Judeo-Christian ethics."

"I know, and I guess we have some things the same, like the Ten Commandments, but our approaches are so different. A Jew is only allowed to give up his life for three things: idolatry, adultery, and murder."

Sondra thought this over as she hung her dress in the closet. "But wouldn't worshipping the devil be idolatry?"

"But they didn't worship the devil."

"That's true."

"Debbie," Mrs. Greenbaum knocked at the door and said something in Yiddish.

"Fine," Debbie replied in English. "Just a minute."

Debbie turned to Sondra. "She wants us to start our showers. Do you want to go first?"

"I'll take my shower in the morning."

Debbie shook her head. "We don't shower on Shabbos."

"Okay," Sondra nervously twisted the turquoise ring that Aunt Irene had brought back from the Grand Canyon for her. "I guess I'll take the first shower."

Later, at the dining room table things did not seem so strange. Mr. Greenbaum sang a few songs and made Kiddush just like her father did at home. After Kiddush, though, everyone was expected to get up and wash their hands.

"Take your ring off your finger and don't say anything after the *bracha* until you swallow the bread," Debbie instructed.

"What bracha?" Sondra asked nervously.

"Don't worry, I'll help you say the blessing." Debbie handed her the washing cup.

71

Debbie's father gave Sondra a reassuring smile and Sondra would have begun to relax if she hadn't noticed the number on Mrs. Greenbaum's arm. For some reason, they hadn't tattooed the workers in Helga's camp, but Debbie's mother apparently had not been so lucky. Sondra willed herself not to look at the brand, but her voice shook as she repeated the blessing after Debbie. Silently she returned to the dining room.

The twisted loaves that Mr. Greenbaum uncovered were different from Helga's homemade bread but just as delicious. Debbie helped her mother serve the soup and later the main course: chicken, tzimmes, salad, and finally sponge cake. Nothing about the meal was that different from the Friday night meals at home. Once the cake was eaten, though, Mrs. Greenbaum apologized for making the meal so rushed.

"Debbie's father has to get back to shul for the services. Now that the days are longer there isn't much time between the real minyan and the eight o'clock one."

"The real minyan?" Sondra questioned.

"The real time to pray Friday night is with sundown," Debbie's father explained.

"Most of the people are not shomer Shabbos," Debbie added. "They want an eight o'clock service after they finish work and have had a nice meal. My father and a few other families daven when they're supposed to."

"Oh, I see," Sondra said, but she really did not.

Debbie passed out little prayer booklets and Sondra saw that everyone was supposed to say the blessing after the meal. At home, her father sang it for everyone.

Later, in Debbie's room, as the two girls sat cross-legged on their beds, Debbie explained some more about her community. There were about a dozen families who were shomer Shabbos and tomorrow morning all of them, except for the Greenbaums, the Marcuses, and the rabbi's family would daven in a little chapel in the basement of the shul.

It wasn't until the following afternoon that Sondra began to see some beauty in being shomer Shabbos. In the morning she woke up with Debbie and dressed quickly. She was surprised to learn that they were not going to eat any breakfast before they left for shul.

"I don't eat 'til after Kiddush," Debbie explained. "You can, though. Do you want some fruit or cake?"

"No," Sondra hesitated. It was clear that Debbie wanted to leave already. Sondra grabbed her purse and threw the strap over her shoulder.

"Don't take your purse," Debbie said.

"Why not? I took all my money out yesterday. It just has tissues in it."

"We don't carry outside the *eruv*, the Shabbos boundary," Debbie said.

Sondra left her purse on the bed and followed her friend. Debbie had the five-block walk to the synagogue well planned out and they crossed from one side of the suburban streets to the other in order to walk under shady trees. Few cars were on the roads and there were even fewer pedestrians until they reached the shul. They met Amy and Anna Goldstein as they pulled open the double doors. Both of the twins had shoulder bags, but then, Sondra assumed, they had probably driven to shul.

Sondra found that she did not have to struggle so hard to follow the services. Afterwards, at the kiddush, she hungrily filled her plate, but before she sat down with Debbie and her friends, she greeted both her aunt and uncle with a kiss and spoke with each of her cousins. When Mr. Greenbaum was ready to leave, she saw that he had a young couple with him. Debbie introduced her and told her that the husband was learning at the Kansas University Medical School.

"They daven downstairs and they come to us a lot for Shabbos meals."

Lunch was not a quick meal like the night before. They sat around the table for a good two hours eating, singing, and discussing the Torah portion as well as politics and community news. Even the food was new to Sondra. There was a stew full of meat, beans, and potatoes that had cooked all night long, which Debbie explained was called *cholent*. The others took heaping portions of it, but Sondra passed it by, feeling safer eating some of the cold chicken left over from dinner.

It was almost three o'clock when they rose from the meal. Debbie's parents walked the guests out and then came back home for their Shabbat naps. Sondra knew there were several more hours left of Shabbat and wondered what they were going to do with all the time.

"Do you want to play backgammon?" Debbie asked.

"I don't know how."

"I can teach you. My brother and I always play when he's home from yeshiva."

"What's that?"

"A school where they learn mainly religious studies."

"Oh, where's his yeshiva?"

"Chicago," Debbie put the game on the dining room table. "This is his last year. Next year he's going to Israel."

"Really?" Sondra was intrigued. Although they had not spoken about it for some time, she still dreamed of traveling to Germany and Israel with Howie.

As Debbie set up the game Sondra found herself telling her the story of the missing Sefer Torah and how her father had gone back to Mafdner and found her mother.

"That's such a cool story," Debbie exclaimed. "Do you know what happened to my father when he went back to his hometown?"

"What?"

"His old neighbors beat him up and told him to get out of town. And that was after the war was over," Debbie added angrily.

"That's terrible."

Debbie nodded and then began explaining the game. They played twice and the second time Sondra won.

"I guess you're a good teacher," Sondra laughed.

Debbie smiled and glanced at the clock. "We're supposed to be at Mr. Marcus's at five. Do you want to play some more or take a nap, or what?"

Sondra had not thought she was tired, but once Debbie mentioned the idea of sleeping it really sounded good.

"Do you usually sleep in the afternoon?"

Debbie laughed. "I just started this past year. My parents always do. There's something in the Shabbos air, or maybe in the cholent, that makes everyone want to sleep."

It was at the Marcuses that Sondra began to understand Debbie's cheerful commitment to all the rules of being shomer Shabbos. Almost all the kids from the ice skating party were there and most of them had walked, but just Debbie, Miriam Schechter, the rabbi's daughter, and David Pines, the son of the family who owned the bakery, were truly shomer Shabbos. The other kids looked up to them and they were natural leaders, telling stories and leading the songs. They spent a pleasant two hours around the Marcuses' table and Sondra had the same feeling she had had at the ice skating party of really belonging.

Later, after *havdalah*, the blessing concluding Shabbat, Mr. Marcus asked Sondra how she had enjoyed the day.

"It was nice," Sondra's eyes sparkled, recalling the singing around the tables both at lunch and at supper. "But I don't understand why there are so many rules. Like does it really make a difference if I tear toilet paper?"

"Oy," Mr. Marcus groaned. "It's a package deal, all the rules. Who knows, if we started tearing the toilet paper we might ruin the whole thing."

"You really think so?" Sondra questioned.

"Yes," Mr. Marcus answered seriously, "I really do."

"I'll have to think about that," Sondra said thoughtfully.

Chapter Eleven

She did a lot of thinking about all the Shabbat rules on the bus ride home, but was soon caught up in summer plans. Shabbat observance was pushed to the back of her mind. The summer was similar to the previous one, except that now, Jane and Christine were already sixteen and had their driver's licenses. Christine's grandparents had even bought her a used Volkswagen and now the girls were independent.

When school started, Mrs. Wiggs announced the musical would be *The Sound of Music.* Sondra was cast as one of the children. Charlie Carson, Howie's best friend, had one of the leads. After the first week of rehearsals, he began offering Sondra rides home in his new, bright red Jaguar. Although she was flattered, Sondra had learned her lesson the year before. Instead of accepting the rides, she suggested he give Joy a lift home. Sondra's friend had gone on a crash diet in the summer and it wasn't long before she and Charlie were going steady. After two years in the drama department, Christine had overcome much of her shyness and was now dating, too. Even Jane was going out. Howie had a new girlfriend, Patty Jenkins, and it didn't look as if he was going to break up with her so quickly. Once the play was over, Sondra found that her friends were really too busy for her. She had plenty of time to study for her midterms and put lots of enthusiasm into working at the store.

The holiday season had just started when she received Debbie's letter about the Winter Convention. It was going to be held in Kansas City from December 26 through December 30. Kids would be there from Omaha, Des Moines, Wichita, and St. Louis. This time there would be no conflicts, no theater, no school, and even working for Uncle Simon would be over. The only problem, Sondra knew, was that she would have to deal with all the Shabbat rules again.

The next day she stopped by her grandmother's and asked her about Shabbat in Germany. The little that Frayda remembered matched what had been done at Debbie's home.

"Why did you stop keeping Shabbos?" Sondra finally asked her grandmother.

"Well," Frayda set her embroidery down. "The boys had to work on Saturday."

"Uncle Simon told them they couldn't have Shabbos off?"

"We never asked him," Frayda said simply. "We were in America and we knew we needed to live like Americans." Frayda took up her handiwork again and changed the subject. "I was thinking that you should start writing down some of my recipes you like so much. I won't be around forever to tell you how to make things. What do you think?"

Sondra dutifully got some paper and a pencil and wrote down half a dozen recipes that Frayda dictated. Once home, even though her arm ached, she wrote an enthusiastic letter to Debbie telling her she would love to come to the convention. She would deal with Shabbat when it came.

Actually, there was really nothing to deal with. Shabbat came and there was no talk about rules. Of course, Sondra noticed, there were no rolls of toilet paper in all of the shul, only the precut kind coming from metal dispensers. And *all* of the lights were taped in every spot of the shul. What there *was* was plenty of singing; singing in the services separate from the main congregation and singing at the meals in the basement. By the time havdalah was made, Sondra had totally forgotten her misgivings. Shabbat was beautiful. What an uplifting experience!

"I feel like I'd like to spend every Shabbos like this," Sondra confided to Brian. The two of them had been sent out to the Safeway to buy some more soda.

"I know the feeling," Brian agreed. He was nice-looking in a Jewish sort of way, with dark, curly hair, a big nose, and glasses. "After every Shabbos meal I spend at the Marcuses, I feel determined to try and keep Shabbos at my house, but somehow Marc and I can't make it work the same. We go to the Pines a lot."

"So you're saying that I won't be able to have the same Shabbos feeling at home?"

"If I were you," Brian smiled, "I would come to Kansas City as much as I could." Sondra smiled back at him, her left dimple deepening. He looked at her the same way Roger and Charlie had looked at her. Only this time, if Brian were to ask her out, she knew that her parents would let her go.

The next three days were full of activities and workshops. Sondra had always thought that now that the Holocaust was over and the State of Israel existed, the Jews had nothing really to worry about. After several of the workshops, she realized how wrong she had been. Perhaps the Jews in America did not have to worry about their rights, but the same was not true for Jews in much of the world, especially in the Soviet Union. And the Israelis were constantly being threatened with terrorist attacks. At Lincoln High there were a number of Afro-American students who advocated Black Pride. By the end of the convention Sondra had decided that she was going to start having Jewish pride.

She tried to explain her feelings to Brian, Debbie, and Marc as they drove her to the Greyhound Bus station.

"It's going to be hard to do by yourself," Marc cautioned.

"You'll have to come to Kansas City a lot to plug in." Brian parked the car.

"You have an open invitation," Debbie added. "My parents really liked having you, and so did I."

Brian took Sondra's suitcase and the three of them walked her to the ticket counter

"I hate to leave," Sondra said as she put her change back in her purse.

"We'll walk you to the bus."

As they went outside the exhaust smell from all the idling buses was overwhelming and it was difficult to talk over all the noise from the motors.

"I guess I should go ahead and get on," Sondra said halfheartedly.

"Come back soon."

Debbie gave Sondra a hug.

"We'll miss you," Debbie yelled as Sondra scrambled up the steps. The bus was only half full and she was able to have a seat by herself. She waved to her friends until they were out of sight and then turned her attention to what was waiting for her at home.

She was pleased that Julius and Helga agreed to her request to go once a month to Kansas City without any problems. Sondra's second goal, to get Howie to go with her, was a different matter.

"I don't want to go to Kansas City next month," Howie declared. Patty was sick and the two of them were sitting together in the lunchroom. "I have a swim meet coming up I have to get ready for."

He did not mention that he was nervous about leaving Patty for the weekend. He knew there were a lot of guys who would be thrilled to take her to the Friday night dance if he was not around. Not only was Patty one of the prettiest girls in the school; she was also one of the nicest. Even Sondra liked her, and Sondra disliked most of his girlfriends on principle.

"Howie," Sondra hesitated, weighing her words carefully, "I learned a lot about being Jewish last week and..."

"I know plenty about Judaism," her cousin interrupted. "Probably more than you do. Don't forget all those bar-mitzvah lessons I went to in Wichita."

Sondra sighed. "I'm not just talking about religious things. I'm talking about being part of the Jewish people."

"So?"

"Look at Stephanie Payne," Sondra pointed to the Afro-American cheerleader. "I remember in eighth grade when they first integrated the school she had her hair straightened so she would look like the white girls. And now she wears it in an Afro and talks about Black Power, and she's just as popular as she was back in junior high."

"What's your point?"

"We have to be proud of who we are."

"Everyone knows we are Jewish. I've never hidden it and neither have you."

"But we should be doing more than not denying it!"

"Like what?"

"I don't know," Sondra faltered for a second or two. "We should be paying more attention to the news. Did you know there was a terror attack on an El Al plane last week?"

Howie shook his head.

"Neither did I. Debbie wrote me about it. No one was killed, so I guess the *Lincoln Daily* didn't think it was worth mentioning. Maybe we should write a letter to the editor complaining."

"Maybe," Howie sounded somewhat interested and Sondra continued.

"Maybe we should start a petition for the Russian ambassador to let the Soviet Jews go. Maybe we should see what we could do to raise money for a project in Israel. Maybe we should start getting serious about our trip to Germany."

"Uh, well," this time Howie faltered, "I've been thinking a lot again about buying a car."

"Really?" Sondra flushed and she felt her eyes fill.

"I don't know." Howie pushed his chair so far back it only rested on two legs. "It seems like the trip was a cute plan for two kids to dream up. Really, how are we going to find a missing Torah somewhere in Europe?"

"Oh."

"If we're really serious we should probably hire a detective."

Sondra nodded. "Okay." She stood up. "I have some homework to finish before my next class. I'll see you in Humanities."

The homework excuse was a lie. Sondra headed to the nearest restroom, locked herself in a stall, and pulled her hurt feelings together. A cute plan for two kids to dream up, indeed. Was she still a kid? The warning bell rang; she washed her face and made it to class on time.

It was Lisa who wanted to talk to Sondra about Jewish identity. The day after Sondra's next weekend in Kansas City, she came out to the farm with Aunt Irene. While their mothers visited together in the kitchen, Sondra filled up a plate of cookies and took her younger cousin up to her room. Lisa was almost a carbon copy of Howie in looks, but where his features were handsome for him, on Lisa they looked decidedly masculine. Sondra hoped her cousin would grow prettier as she matured. In spite of her looks, Lisa was bright and outgoing and always had plenty of friends. However, her best friend was her cousin, Rachel. The two girls wrote weekly letters back and forth, spent a week at each other's homes every summer, and on special occasions were even allowed to call one another.

"Did you see Rachel?" Lisa asked eagerly.

"At shul," Sondra answered.

"Did she cut her hair yet?"

Sondra thought for a moment and nodded.

"Does it look nice?"

"Uh-hum. Have another cookie."

"Thanks." Lisa took several. "I'm thinking of getting mine cut, too. What do you think?"

Sondra studied her cousin's bushy ponytail. "It might be nice, a short curly cut."

Lisa nodded. "I think I'll do it. Tell me, Sondra, how come you never had a bat mitzvah?"

Surprised Sondra shrugged her shoulders. "I never thought about it. Bernice didn't have one. No one did."

"Rachel did."

"I guess so, I guess that was a bat mitzvah." Sondra recalled how they had all driven in three carloads to Kansas City for Friday night services last year. The only thing Rachel had done was read the haftarah in English and make a two-minute speech at the end of the services. Afterwards there had been an oneg Shabbat, a gathering with singing and refreshments in the shul. What Sondra remembered most about the whole trip was that Debbie had not been at the services and how disappointed she had been.

"I want to have a bat mitzvah."

"But you're already twelve."

"My cousin in Chicago is having one when she's thirteen and I want one, too." Lisa spoke decidedly.

"Oh."

"She's reading from the Torah just like Howie did and I want to do that, too."

"It's only in the Reform shuls that girls read from the Torah," Sondra said softly.

"Well," Lisa folded her arms on her chest, "we're like a Reform shul here. We use a Reform prayer book."

"What do your parents think?"

Lisa made a face. "They're still talking about it. That's why I wanted to talk to you."

Sondra took another cookie and waited.

"I want you to tell my parents how much you've always regretted not having a bat mitzvah."

Sondra laughed. "But I don't regret it. I never thought about it until now."

"Why do you always have to be such a goody-goody?" Lisa asked angrily.

"What?" This time Sondra stifled her laugh.

"You always do what your parents want. Do you have any

idea all the stuff Howie gets away with? And he gets away with a lot just because he's the boy."

"You sound jealous, Lisa," Sondra tried to keep the impatience out of her voice.

"Of course I'm jealous. Howie dates non-Jewish girls, he gets the car whenever he wants, and he doesn't have a curfew. I can't go round the block without asking permission. And when I want to do something to show I'm Jewish my parents hem and haw as if I'd asked for a trip to Europe." Lisa brushed an angry tear off her cheek.

"I'm sorry," Sondra put an arm around her cousin's shoulder. "I'm glad you care about being Jewish, though. There're things you and I can do together besides having a bat mitzvah to show we care."

"Like what?"

Sondra took a deep breath. "Like writing letters to our congressmen asking them to put pressure on Russia to let the Jews out so they can move to Israel."

"You mean they can't leave Russia if they want?" Lisa asked.

Sondra took several minutes to give Lisa a crash course about the Refuseniks, and when she finished, Lisa seemed interested.

"Lisa, let's go," Aunt Irene called from the bottom of the stairs.

"I still want a bat mitzvah," Lisa declared as she put on her coat.

"I hope you get one," Sondra answered as she walked her cousin to the door.

Chapter Twelve

*L*isa was ecstatic when she called Sondra a week later and told her that her parents had agreed to a bat mitzvah.

"Daddy's taking me to Wichita tomorrow to meet with the rabbi."

"I'm happy for you," Sondra said.

"I think I'll ask the rabbi about the Soviet Jews."

"Good idea," Sondra answered. She planned to ask Mr. Marcus for addresses on her next trip to Kansas City.

She stayed with Debbie again and, without being reminded, put all of her *muktza* items in her purse and stowed the purse under her bed. After havdalah, before the bowling party, Mr. Marcus looked over the sample letter she and Lisa had written up. He made a few minor corrections and on Monday, after school, Sondra and Lisa took turns working on Herbert's typewriter in the basement. Howie returned from swim practice and offered to help. His typing was much faster than both of the girls' and in no time they were finished.

Afterwards, they sat around the kitchen table and sipped hot chocolate and addressed the envelopes. There was a nice camaraderie among the three of them. It was the first time that Lisa could remember that Howie and Sondra were together and did not treat her like a pest.

"Were you scared when you got up on the stage at your bar mitzvah?" she suddenly asked her brother.

"Not at all."

"How about you?" Lisa turned to Sondra. "Were you scared when you were in *The King and I*?"

"I was terrified the first few minutes and then I was okay. Are you already getting nervous about the bat mitzvah?"

"A little bit," Lisa admitted.

"I don't believe you!" Howie threw his arms in the air. "You nagged and nagged about wanting a bat mitzvah and now you're scared."

"I didn't say I was scared," Lisa responded with dignity. "I said I was nervous. There's a difference."

"You're right," Howie conceded. "Don't worry. The rabbi is going to make you practice your Torah portion so often you'll be able to do it in your sleep."

In less than a month they had received replies from all of the congressmen. Although the letters were sympathetic, it was clear that the war in Vietnam and the protests against it were what held the attention of most of the politicians. Sondra was at the spring play practice when she heard the news about Kent State. National Guardsmen, who had been called in to control the anti-war protests, had shot and killed four students on the Ohio college campus.

It was Roger who announced the news. Although more than a year had passed since he had asked Sondra to the prom, she was still sensitive to his emotions. She noticed that his face had turned pale.

"I'm going to Kent State next year." His voice was shaky.

"Maybe you should change your plans," Charlie joked, but no one laughed.

"I can't believe kids could get murdered just walking on campus," Christine spoke softly.

"Who says they were just walking?" one of the freshmen

snapped. "The National Guard was there because of all the pro-tests, and some of them were violent."

A few of the kids agreed with the freshman, but most did not. Voices were raised and the discussion became heated. Mrs. Wiggs called an end to play practice and sent everyone home.

By the next day it was clear from the news that only one of the students had been protesting. All of the others had been on their way to classes; one of them had even been going to his ROTC class. The mood at play practice was one of indignation, but Mrs. Wiggs was able to maintain control. Later, as they walked out to the parking lot, Sondra found herself deep in discussion with Jane, Roger, and two other seniors.

"We should have a memorial service for the slain students," one of the girls said.

Roger nodded his head. "I'm going to speak to the principal tomorrow at lunch break. Does anyone want to go with me?"

"I have an orthodontist appointment during lunch," Jane shook her head.

"I have a paper to finish," the girl with the suggestion excused herself.

"Sorry, Roger," the other senior answered. "I had words with Dr. Martin last week. I don't think I'll be an asset."

"I'll go with you," Sondra said quietly and found herself blushing when Roger gave her a grateful smile.

As Dr. Martin ushered them into his office Sondra thought how appropriate it was for Roger to be the spokesman. With his conservative clothes and haircut he looked nothing like a typical war protester. Surely the principal would listen to him. He did. Dr. Martin sat patiently with his hands folded in front of him and gave Roger his full attention. Once Roger finished Dr. Martin unfolded his hands and placed them palm down on his desk.

"Those students were killed on a college campus. We're a high school. How is that relevant to the student body?"

"Well, sir," Roger's voice was full of confidence, "a good percentage of the student body will be going to college next year and, frankly, we're a little scared."

Dr. Martin nodded and drummed his fingers on his desk for a full five minutes. Finally he nodded.

"Okay, we'll let school out ten minutes early on Friday. Whoever wants to stay for the service can. You can have the auditorium."

Roger displayed none of the disappointment he felt, but he made one request.

"We'd prefer to use the courtyard of the school, sir, if that's okay."

Dr. Martin nodded his head and the two shook hands cordially.

Sondra, who had not made a sound throughout the interchange, followed Roger silently out of the office. Once the door was closed behind them Roger slammed his fist into the palm of his hand.

"Ten minutes! Wow! I hope if I get killed in college next year they'll give me more than ten minutes."

"We can make it as long as we want," Sondra pointed out as they entered the cafeteria.

"Yeah, but the bus students will have to leave as soon as the bell rings."

"I didn't think about that," Sondra admitted and fell silent. She felt totally inadequate to deal with her own emotions, much less Roger's. The picture in her mind of the innocent students being gunned down by National Guardsmen was too similar to the dozens of pictures she had in her mind of Jews being gunned down by Nazis. The only way she could think of fighting the injustice was to help with the memorial service.

There was a meeting called for that afternoon in the library. To Sondra's chagrin, she found that everyone else there were seniors. Plus, she happened to overhear that Roger had just broken up with his girlfriend. She hoped he didn't think she was chasing him. Embarrassed, she sat tongue-tied and left as quickly as she could. She didn't go to the other meeting and told Roger that between homework and play practice she had no time. She did stay for the memorial service on Friday, though. The courtyard was crowded as almost all the seniors and half of the other students were there. Four students held crosses with the names of the slain students on them. Poems were read and everyone stood for a minute of silence while one of the boys played taps on his trumpet. Roger and the others had done a good job. The service was short and moving, but Sondra felt like an outsider and went home feeling depressed.

Finding a blue envelope in the mailbox when she arrived raised her spirits a bit. Debbie's letters were always a treat and surely she would have something comforting to say about Kent State. Eagerly Sondra tore open the letter and read it as she walked up the path to the house. What her friend had written, though, only shocked Sondra. Calling a quick hello to her mother she ran up the stairs to her room and dialed her cousin's number.

"Howie," Sondra spoke breathlessly, "do you know that three of the students killed at Kent State were Jewish?"

"Really?"

"That's what Debbie wrote."

"Some of those names did sound Jewish," Howie admitted.

"Yeah. And here they held crosses for them!"

"Don't get so upset," Howie's voice sounded so calm. "Originally the cross was just a symbol of death, not Christianity."

"You think it was okay to hold a cross for them?"

"I did not say that," Howie stated firmly. "But what's done is done. We can just comfort ourselves by thinking of it as a symbol of death."

"Well, okay. But if I ever get killed you make sure no one holds a cross for me."

"We'll see who goes first," Howie laughed.

Sondra laughed halfheartedly in return. The fact that the students were Jewish made her analogy to the Nazis gunning down Jews so much more apt. She spent the weekend brooding over the issue. Full of questions, she wondered whether Jews really belonged in America. For the first time she contemplated going to Israel for university, but dismissed the idea knowing her parents would not want her to go so far away. On Monday morning, though, she resolutely pushed her depression away. Play practice, term papers, end of the year examinations, and helping with the bat mitzvah were ahead of her. There would be no time for moping.

Chapter Thirteen

*A*lthough Lisa's birthday was in the middle of June, one week after school was out, her parents decided to celebrate her bat mitzvah on July 3rd. Friday night would be for Lisa and Saturday, Independence Day, would, of course, be Uncle Simon's day. More out-of-town relatives would come, since there would be two occasions to come for. Irene thought the plan was perfect.

Things don't always go as planned, though.

Sondra's pink Princess phone woke her several minutes after six in the morning the second day of summer vacation. Before she could lift her head off the pillow the ringing stopped. Curious, though, Sondra pulled her robe on and made her way down the stairs, to the kitchen. The room was bright with sunshine and the smell of melted butter saturated the air. Helga stood frozen, her back to the stove, an open egg in her hand, trying to guess who was on the other end of the phone. Julius had taken his milking cap off his head and was wiping his brow with it.

"Uh-huh…I see…Yes, I'll call Herbert…No, I'll drive over to Mama's as soon as I clean up…I'm sorry…Of course."

Julius hung the phone up slowly and turned to face his women.

"That was Berta. Her father died peacefully in his sleep."

Helga put her hands to her mouth. "Poor Berta."

"How's Aunt Sopha?" Sondra asked.

"I'm not sure she understands."

"When's the funeral going to be?"

"Tomorrow."

"What's this going to do to Lisa's bat mitzvah?" Sondra asked her mother as Julius dialed the phone.

"That's for Irene and Herbert to decide." Helga spoke more sharply than she intended. Although her first response had been one of sympathy for Berta, she really envied her. She had had her father for sixty years. She would know the date of the anniversary of his death and be able to visit his grave. Helga stared at the egg in her hand and threw it into the frying pan. She quickly added five more. Just because Uncle Eli had died there was no reason for them to starve.

The Jewish section of the Lincoln cemetery was on a little plot of land that Uncle Simon had bought years earlier when Mamie died. There were only eight graves there and most of them were relatives. Sondra had been there once before, at her grandfather's funeral. Then it had been spring and the pastureland that surrounded the cemetery on three sides had been in full bloom. There had been a slight breeze and Sondra had worn a light jacket. Now the air was still and even though it was only ten o'clock in the morning, the sun was beating down on the small crowd gathered around the open grave.

Bernice had come in the night before. Several months pregnant, she had her hands full with her mother.

"Oh, if only Alfred was alive," Berta sobbed. "Then he could say *kaddish* for Papa."

Sondra stared at her older cousin. Was this the same businesslike Berta who never seemed to show her emotions or care about religious issues? Was it really so important to her that someone say the memorial prayer for her father?

"Don't worry, Berta," Uncle Simon spoke softly. "I'll say kaddish for my brother."

"Poor Uncle Simon," Sondra thought. This was the second younger brother he was burying.

After the services the family went back to Berta's house to eat the mourning meal. Again Berta lamented the absence of her brother.

"Mama," Bernice tried to comfort her mother, "Uncle Simon is Opa's brother. A brother can say kaddish, too."

"He's saying it today. But what about tomorrow and the next day and the next? When is he going to be at a minyan? Once a month?"

"Will it make you feel better," Bernice asked, "if I ask Robert's uncle to arrange for someone to say kaddish for Opa every day?"

"Yes, it would." Berta dried her eyes and began to eat from the food on the table. It was not long before she had her equilibrium back and was bantering with the relatives.

Sondra watched it all, amazed at the mood swings Berta was having. Now that her mother was calm, Bernice rose from her place and pulled up a chair next to Sondra.

"How are things at Lincoln High?"

"Fine," Sondra smiled. Despite Bernice's pregnant stomach and wedding ring, she was still the same Bernice.

"You're becoming quite an actress, I understand."

Sondra blushed. "It's a lot of fun."

"Are you thinking about doing anything with it?"

"I've thought some about children's theater, drama education." Sondra spoke diffidently.

"Have you started thinking about colleges?"

"Not really."

Bernice laid a hand on her cousin's shoulder. "Don't go to Lincoln State."

"That's what my parents say."

"Listen to them," Bernice instructed. "I grew up here and Robin Cohen and I were the only practicing Jews in the whole high school. When I got to Oklahoma University I couldn't believe it. It seemed like almost every other person I met was Jewish. It was a whole new world. And it's the same in Philadelphia. I have a community that I belong to."

"I know what you mean," Sondra answered. She explained to Bernice how good she felt being with the Kansas City youth group.

"That's great," Bernice nodded. "This summer is the time for you to start thinking about colleges. Talk to your friends in Kansas City and find out where they want to go. Go with some of them."

"Maybe I will," Sondra nodded. However, she could not see herself going all the way to New York like Debbie was going to do. She wondered what colleges Howie was considering. She would have to talk to him about it. They did not talk as much as they used to. Howie was still going steady with Patty, but Sondra noticed that he had not bought a car yet.

The following afternoon, when Helga knew that Howie and Lisa would be at the pool, she stopped by Irene's. As the two women settled down at the kitchen table with their cups of coffee, Irene surveyed her kitchen with satisfaction. There were no dishes in the sink, the counters were clear, and the floor swept. Dinner was all ready to put in the oven. She deserved a half-hour of gossip with her sister-in-law.

"So," Helga didn't mince words, "what is happening with the bat mitzvah plans?"

Irene shook her head. "Herbert and I were up till all hours deciding what to do. Lisa's still going to have her bat mitzvah, but instead of the dinner we had planned to host beforehand, we'll just have a simple oneg Shabbat at the house afterwards."

"How does Lisa feel about it?"

Irene smiled. "She thought the whole thing was going to be canceled, so she's happy."

"Good," Helga nodded. "How did she react to the funeral?"

"Very quiet. What about Sondra?"

"She picked up on what Berta said about Eli not having a son to say kaddish for him. She wanted to know who would say kaddish for Julius and me. And it bothered her that kaddish wasn't said for Julius's father on a regular basis."

"Oh." Irene made a face. "That must not have been pleasant." She stood up and brought a fruit bowl to the table.

Helga helped herself to a peach and changed the subject. "Is all the family still coming in?"

"I think so. Bernice is going to stay until afterwards. Her mother can use her and Robert will come in as planned." Irene took a long swallow. "Howie wants to invite his girlfriend."

"It's that serious?"

"I'm worried."

Helga circled the rim of her coffee cup with her index finger. "Do you ever feel like we should pick up and move someplace that has a real shul and Jewish community?"

Irene sighed and rested her chin on her folded hands in front of her. "It was fine here when the kids were young. I mean, I think we gave them a real Jewish identity. I know Herbert taught the kids to read Hebrew and I taught them about the holidays…"

"Julius did the same with Sondra."

"I know." Irene nodded and rubbed her eyes. "It's just so hard in high school with all the dating and parties."

"From what Julius told me," Helga disagreed, "he never got caught up in it. And neither did Lotte."

"Neither did Herbert, for that matter. And from what I understood, neither did Berta or Alfred or even Uncle Nathan's girls. But that was a different time."

"You're right," Helga nodded. "And I guess that we're stuck here."

"We are. We just better keep working on the kids' Jewish identity. It's good that you're sending Sondra to Kansas City so much. I wish I could get Howie to want to go."

"I'll speak to Sondra about it. They're not together as much as they used to be, but they still talk."

"Maybe she can find him a girl in Kansas City," Irene laughed.

Chapter Fourteen

*I*n the end, Patty was invited to the bat mitzvah on condition that Howie go with Sondra and Lisa when they went to Lotte's for a week in the middle of July. Irene and Herbert were hoping for the very thing that Howie feared – that once he was away, Patty would find someone else.

Sondra had overheard enough talks between her mother and her aunt to know that was the plan, but she did not think it was very likely to happen. She had watched Patty carefully at the oneg Shabbat. Simply dressed in a sleeveless, yellow dress that showed off her beautiful tan, Patty had spent most of the evening sitting by herself. She had not taken her eyes off Howie as he visited with guests and endured being photographed. As she watched him, she played with his ID bracelet that she wore on her left wrist. Feeling sorry for her, and against her better judgment, Sondra had finally sat down next to her.

"Are you having a nice time?"

Patty smiled brightly and nodded her head.

"I've never seen anything like this."

"Like what?"

"A Jewish religious service. The food." Patty held up a cracker spread with chopped liver. "So many people speaking with foreign accents. My family has lived in Kansas since before the Civil War."

"What do they think of you being here?" Sondra could not keep herself from asking.

Patty pulled at a lock of her waist-length blonde hair and twisted it around her forefinger. "They feel the same way your aunt and uncle would probably feel if I took Howie to communion with me."

"I'm sorry," Sondra blushed. "I guess that was a nosy question." To her surprise Patty laughed.

"You just asked what everyone else wants to ask. I appreciate your being honest."

Howie had joined them at that point, and although he told Sondra to stay, she saw that Patty had eyes only for her steady, so she left to help Aunt Irene pass the cake trays.

Howie and Patty spent practically every waking moment together the following week, in preparation for their weeklong separation. Howie was not at all enthusiastic about the trip to Kansas City, but knowing Patty would be at her grandmother's for the same week made him resolve to make the best of it.

Irene had decided to make the drive to Lotte's into a day vacation. She insisted on stopping in Topeka and taking the kids to see the state capitol building. As long as they were stopping there, Herbert suggested that they should eat lunch at The Place. He had heard about the steak restaurant at the cattle auctions and if anyone was a good judge of a steak place, it was a cattleman. Herbert had been told that although The Place was totally without atmosphere, the prices were low and the food fantastic.

Everything Herbert had been told was true. The five of them sat around a plain wooden table without a tablecloth or placemats. The menus were spattered with grease and the waitress stood impatiently, without a smile, while waiting for them to order.

Herbert cleared his throat. "My wife would like the filet mignon but without the bacon, the baked potato, and the salad. Lisa, you want a hamburger, right?"

Lisa nodded. "And I want French fries and coleslaw."

Without a comment, the waitress scribbled on her pad.

"What about you, Sondra?" her uncle asked.

"Um, can I have the baked sole?"

"Sondra," Herbert was irritated, "this is a steak house, not a fish restaurant…"

"Herbert," Irene interrupted, "let the girl order what she wants."

Herbert grunted in response. As soon as the waitress finished with the order he turned his attention to his niece.

"Why didn't you order a steak?" he demanded.

Sondra played with her ring and did not look at her uncle. "I don't eat meat out anymore."

Herbert shook his head. "It's very nice you care about being Jewish, but don't carry it too far. You know," he pointed his finger at Sondra, "you need to be like Bernice. She married a nice Jewish boy, she has a kosher home, they go to a nice shul. Don't be a fanatic."

Before Sondra could reply the drinks arrived and Aunt Irene changed the subject. Nothing more was said about Sondra's lunch choice, but she ate quietly and was rather uncomfortable as they toured the Menniger Center. Howie, sensitive to his cousin's discomfort, kept the conversation going in the back seat for the hour ride from Topeka to Kansas City. Still, Sondra was glad when Lotte's ranch house came into view.

Aunt Lotte had a list of activities planned for her nieces and nephew, but there was still going to be time for Sondra to see Debbie, and, she hoped, Brian and the others.

"Can I call Debbie?" Sondra asked her aunt once Aunt Irene and Uncle Herbert had said goodbye.

"Sure," Aunt Lotte replied. "She was asking about you yesterday."

"So was Brian," Rachel grinned, and Sondra blushed.

"You can use the phone in my room," Aunt Lotte said. "Maybe you'll have some privacy there."

Debbie was as anxious to see Sondra as Sondra was to see her.

"My aunt has all sorts of plans for us this week," Sondra explained. "But she said I could invite you along. Do you want to go downtown with us? We're going to the concert at the park."

"No, it's the Three Weeks."

"The three weeks?"

"Never mind, I'll explain when we get together. What are the plans for tomorrow?"

"We're going swimming at the JCC."

"Great. I'll meet you there."

"You got your braces off!" Sondra shrieked when they met at the pool the following day.

"How do you like my smile?" Debbie grinned widely.

"Great!"

"Come, let's change into our swimsuits." Debbie led the way.

"Is your brother here?" Sondra asked.

"No," Debbie replied. "He's still in yeshiva, but even if he was home he wouldn't be here. He doesn't go mixed swimming."

"I don't see any Afro-Americans here." Sondra looked around.

"Not that kind of mixed swimming," Debbie laughed.

"Then what?"

"Boys and girls." The two girls entered dressing rooms next to each other.

"Why can't boys and girls go swimming together?" Sondra called over the partition.

"His rabbi told him it wasn't modest," Debbie called back.

She exited the stall with a towel draped over her one-piece bathing suit. Sondra came out also wrapped in a towel. They looked at each other and laughed.

"I feel half naked walking from here to the pool in just a swimsuit."

"Me too."

"So how come you go mixed swimming?" Sondra asked the obvious question.

"My parents let me, so I'm not going to ask any questions," Debbie shrugged. "Especially in this heat."

The girls left their towels at the side of the crowded Olympic-sized pool and jumped into the water.

"Is everyone here Jewish?" Sondra asked amazed after swimming several laps.

"Most of them, but not all," Debbie shook her head.

"That's my cousin," Sondra pointed to Howie who was swimming towards them.

As he drew close he tried to dunk Sondra, who pushed him with all her might. He laughed in her face and splashed her.

"Who's your friend?"

"This is Debbie," Sondra answered and noticed Howie looking with interest at Debbie's green eyes. Sondra's imagination immediately began working. Suppose Howie would be interested in Debbie and he would break up with Patty? It would be wonderful. Before Sondra could begin imagining being the bridesmaid at the wedding, though, she remembered that Debbie's parents did not let her date.

Later, as they sat on the grass, wrapped again in their towels, Sondra asked Debbie why she hadn't been able to go to the concert the day before.

"It's the three weeks before Tisha b'Av. Do you know what that is?"

Sondra shook her head. Apparently that holiday had been left off the list her father had taught her about.

"It's the date that the first and second *Beit Hamikdash*, the Holy Temple in Jerusalem, were destroyed. Do you know about the Temple?"

Sondra explained about Mr. Mane's phone call following the Six-Day War.

Debbie nodded. "The Beit Hamikdash was the holiest place on earth. All we have left of it is the Kotel, the Western Wall."

"I remember the picture of the soldiers praying there."

Debbie nodded again. "But it's just one wall. We need the whole Beit Hamikdash. So every year on the ninth of Av we fast and mourn for it."

"I thought we only fast on Yom Kippur."

Debbie shook her head. "Maybe Reform Jews only fast on Yom Kippur, but religious Jews fast several times a year."

"Really?" Sondra was skeptical, but let it go. "What does all this have to do with going to a concert?"

"Oh, for the three weeks before Tisha b'Av we're not supposed to hear any live music."

"Really?" Before Sondra could ask another question someone stepped up behind her and covered her eyes with his hands. "Guess who?"

Sondra pulled the hands down and turned to see Brian smiling at her. Her face lit up and she invited him and Marc to join her and Debbie. It was fun, almost like being on a double date. And later, when Marc and Debbie went back in the water, Brian really asked her for a date.

"There's a nice play showing at The Starlight Theater Thursday night. Would you like to go with me?"

"I'd love too, if it's okay with my aunt. Which play?"

"*Barefoot in the Park.*"

"Neil Simon is one of my favorite playwrights."

At that point Howie, straight from the pool, plopped down next to her.

"Howie, this is Brian Cohen. Brian, this is my cousin, Howie."

The two boys shook hands and tried to size each other up. Howie assumed, correctly, that Brian was not very interested in sports and Brian surmised that Howie was a jock.

"Are you a senior?" Howie asked.

Brian shook his head. "I graduated last month. I'm going to the University of Colorado in Boulder."

"So, you made a decision," Sondra commented. She sure

would miss Brian when she came to Kansas City during the school year. Maybe she would look into Boulder. Bernice had told her to try to find a university where some of her friends were going.

"Sondra!"

Sondra smiled at three of the kids from the youth group. "Come meet my cousin Howie."

She made the introductions as Marc and Debbie returned. One of the boys had a big bag of potato chips. He fixed his yarmulke on his head, said a blessing, and passed the bag around.

"Where's Miriam?" Sondra asked.

"She doesn't go mixed swimming either," Debbie answered.

"Don't forget she's the rabbi's daughter," one of the girls added.

Howie looked at Sondra for an explanation, but she just shrugged her shoulders.

He saw a lot of new things that afternoon. The camaraderie between Sondra's friends was deep and it seemed to center on Jewish issues.

"We're having a letter-writing campaign tomorrow night, if you'd like to come," Marc told him.

"Letter writing for what?"

"Soviet Jews."

"Yeah," Howie answered decisively, "I'd like to come. What about you, Sondra?"

"Of course."

When they entered Mr. Marcus's home the following evening, the gang was spread out on the living room floor with pads of paper in front of them and bowls of popcorn and Chex cereal mix scattered on the carpet. To Howie, they all looked like normal teenagers, except for the yarmulkes on the boys' heads. They wrote for over an hour and then stopped, complaining of writer's cramp. Brian suggested a game of charades and they played for another hour until Mrs. Marcus signaled that it was time for them to leave.

"She just tolerates us for her husband's sake," Debbie whispered to Sondra on the way out. "And he's so good to us that we don't ever overstay our welcome."

"What did you think of everyone?" Sondra asked her cousin as they parted from the others and walked home.

"They're nice kids." Howie nodded. "Brian told me that he plans on majoring in pre-law. I think he's interested in you."

Sondra blushed and tried not to let Howie see her smile.

"I guess your folks wouldn't mind you dating him."

"He's taking me out Thursday night."

"How about that," Howie commented, happy for his cousin. They walked in a comfortable silence past several houses. There was a smell of rain in the air and occasional sparks of lightning. A summer storm was on its way.

"Everyone wants me to break up with Patty," Howie broke the silence.

"You're right," Sondra agreed. "They would not be so worried if she wasn't so nice. You know that."

"I guess that's supposed to make me feel better." Howie spoke ruefully. "Sondra, I really care about her a lot."

Sondra heard the emotion in her cousin's voice and felt a stab of fear. It was not that unusual in Lincoln for senior couples to get married right after high school. She groped for the right thing to say.

"Howie, you were my first friend, my best friend, and I never want to hurt you or make you mad at me." Sondra hesitated.

"Go on." Howie slowed his pace.

"You have two sides to you. The Jewish side that wants to find the Torah and visit Israel, and the other side that wants to be the captain of the football team and date the head cheerleader. They don't really go together, at least in Lincoln, where none of the cheerleaders are Jewish."

"You're the only one in the drama department who is Jewish."

"Don't get angry. It's not the same. I've made the Jewish things top priority. They can't be equal. And I'm not interested in dating anyone from the drama department."

"You were."

Sondra stopped and faced her cousin. "I made a mistake. My parents' sending me to Kansas City was the best thing that could have happened to me. Maybe you should start coming with me when I come."

"Maybe," Howie said halfheartedly. "I think it might be a little late for that, though. I really care a lot about Patty," he repeated.

"Have you started thinking about college?" Sondra asked.

"Lincoln State has one of the best veterinary schools. I might just stay at home."

"I suppose that's what Patty's planning to do, too," Sondra said sadly.

"Probably," Howie admitted.

That night, after saying the *shema*, which her parents had taught her to say every night before she went to sleep, Sondra prayed with all her might for something to happen to make Howie break up with Patty.

Chapter Fifteen

*A*s the plane took off, Sondra gripped the armrests, squeezing them so tightly that the veins in her hands stood out.

"Relax," Helga told her daughter softly. "Watch how everything down below changes into a miniature world."

Sondra did as instructed and she felt herself relax. It was the Tuesday before Thanksgiving and Uncle Herbert had dropped her and her mother off at Wichita Airport to catch a flight to Denver. From there they would take a taxi to Boulder to check out the university. Tomorrow they would fly into Kansas City and Julius would meet them there on Thursday for a turkey dinner.

The University of Colorado was the third college that had accepted Sondra. The deadline for sending in her registration money was fast approaching and, even though U of C was her first choice, her parents did not want her making a final decision until she had seen the campus. If all went well, Brian would be there to meet them and show them around.

Even before they reached the campus, Sondra fell in love with the mountains.

"It's a little like Mafdner," Helga had remarked.

As Brian gave them a tour, Sondra paid close attention to the campus population. Most were dressed in jeans and about every third student had wire-rim glasses. Sondra did not notice one jock, but she did see several yarmulkes. Posters plastered all over the Student Union showed that the University of Colorado campus was one with a social conscience. Although the Hillel rabbi was already on his Thanksgiving vacation, they stopped by the Union of Jewish Students and Brian showed off the kosher kitchen facilities.

"The rabbi is Orthodox," he told her. "The Shabbos services are just like the basement at Ohev Shalom."

Sondra was convinced that this was where she wanted to spend the next four years of her life and she told Brian so later that evening when the two of them went out for a walk.

He squeezed her hand in approval and then did not let go. Sondra knew that Mr. Marcus would not approve of her and Brian holding hands, but he wasn't there.

"How did *Fiddler on the Roof* go?" Brian asked.

Sondra nodded her head enthusiastically. "Mrs. Wiggs knows how to get the best out of us."

"This was your biggest part, wasn't it?"

Again, Sondra nodded. They wandered into a coffeehouse where someone was playing a guitar and singing folk music.

"Marc's almost as good as him," Brian said, but they sat down anyway and ordered coffee.

"You know, doing the play made me realize how little I really know about being Jewish."

"Hum?"

"Like Mrs. Wiggs told us we should put our fingers to the doorpost every time we went in and out of a building as if we were kissing the *mezuzah*. One of the girls asked me about it and when I told her I didn't do it at home she was shocked. And I felt embarrassed."

"There's lots of Christians who don't do everything they're supposed to," Brian answered sympathetically.

"I guess so." Sondra played with her spoon. "Debbie told me there are lots of Jews who do kiss the mezuzah every time they go in and out of their houses."

"I know," Brian nodded. "I have cousins in New York who

are ultra-Orthodox. They kiss the mezuzahs and the boys learn in yeshiva for years and years and they almost never speak to a non-Jew. They don't celebrate Thanksgiving or the Fourth of July. They don't even have a TV." Brian shook his head. "It's not for me."

"So," Sondra asked, "what is for you?"

"Shabbos and keeping kosher," Brian answered without a moment's hesitation. "What about you?"

Sondra hesitated, obviously far less sure of herself than Brian. "I guess I'm a little two-faced. I keep Shabbos in Kansas City but not really in Lincoln."

"I told you it's hard to do by yourself."

"You did," Sondra nodded. "And you were right. Most Friday nights, except when there was the play, I manage okay. My father always makes Kiddush and my mother bakes her own challahs and, unless we have services at the university, I read with my nightstand light that I keep on all Shabbos. But during the day it's different. And next week I have to work at the store."

"For the holiday season?"

"Yes. My uncle told both Howie and me way back in the summer that he was counting on us for Saturdays and after school."

"How's your cousin?"

"Okay," Sondra sighed.

"He's still dating that girl?"

Sondra nodded. "What you said about your cousins almost never speaking to a non-Jew sounds good to me. Everything is changing at home. My best friend, Jane, has become a born-again Christian and only wants to talk about Jesus. And another friend, Joy, is about as serious with Howie's best friend as Howie is with Patty. Another friend, Christine, moved away."

A waiter passed their table with a tray of hamburgers, French fries, and drinks.

"Smells good," Brian commented and Sondra nodded in agreement.

"Do you want to order something?"

"You eat out?" Sondra was puzzled.

"Fresh salads and fruit and ice cream."

"Oh," Sondra spoke thoughtfully. "You know, until I met Debbie and Mr. Marcus I thought keeping kosher just meant having a kosher house and not eating pork or shellfish."

"Too bad it's not that easy," Brian laughed.

Helga was watching the end of an old movie when Sondra returned to the hotel room.

"Did you have a nice walk?" she asked absently.

"Yes, I did." Sondra busied herself getting ready for bed.

A few minutes later the movie ended. Helga clicked off the TV and brushed the sentimental tears off her cheeks.

"Brian seems like a nice boy." Helga's tone was offhand and her back was to Sondra as she searched for her nightgown in the suitcase.

"Yes, he is. He's just as nice as Roger Morris."

Helga turned from the suitcase and faced her daughter. "That is so nice of you to tell me that." Again there were tears in her eyes. "When I told you that you couldn't go out with Roger, I was afraid that you were going to hate me for the rest of your life."

"Oh, Mommy." Tears welled up in Sondra's eyes. "I would never hate you."

"Maybe not," Helga smiled. "But you sure were angry at me."

"I was. At the beginning. Everything worked out for the best, though."

"Yes," Helga gave her daughter a hug. "Oh, I sure am going to miss you next year."

"Do you," Sondra hesitated, "do you want me to go to Lincoln State?"

"Definitely not!" Helga pulled back from Sondra and shook her head emphatically.

"Okay," Sondra laughed. "Don't worry. I don't want to go there either. Even though it's a fine university. I can't believe that we're graduating the same year."

"I put a lot of years into my Ph.D. I hope you never felt neglected by it."

"No, Mom, never," Sondra shook her head. "Have they decided how many courses you're going to teach next year?"

"Just two." Sondra could hear the disappointment in her mother's voice. "There's not enough funding for a Holocaust Studies Department yet."

Sondra pulled down her blanket and began brushing her hair in bed. Keeping her voice as casual as possible and with her heart beating madly, she made the suggestion that she had been thinking of for the past month.

"Maybe you should collect the reparations money from Germany and use that for funding."

"Maybe," Helga said guardedly. If she wondered how Sondra knew she had never applied for the compensation, she did not ask.

The next morning, before leaving Boulder, Helga and Sondra made their way to the Registrar's Office. Helga paid the registration fee and Sondra requested the dorm she wanted.

"Good luck," the middle-aged secretary smiled and Sondra felt a surge of excitement at the decision she had just made. She spent most of the flight to Kansas City daydreaming about the upcoming year. Helga was also preoccupied with thoughts about the lectures that she would be teaching the following year. They were both quiet, but it was a pleasant quiet and they were in good spirits when Lotte met them at the airport.

"You're becoming quite a world traveler," Julius teased his daughter as he and Helga got ready to leave Kansas City on Thursday afternoon. Lotte had purposely had a noon Thanksgiving dinner so her brother could get home in time to milk the cows. Sondra was staying on, though, until Sunday morning, with Debbie.

"I would not call traveling to two states a world traveler," Uncle Manny laughed.

"Speaking of world travelers," Sondra took a deep breath. "Some of the seniors here are thinking of going to Israel this summer on a tour. I would love to go with them. What do you think?"

It was Helga who broke the silence that had met Sondra's request.

"I guess you've given your father and me something to talk about on the drive home."

"It's none of my business," Lotte said, "but I think it would be a wonderful opportunity for Sondra."

"You're right, Lotte," Julius said kindly. "It isn't any of your business. There's a lot for Helga and me to think about. Don't worry, sweetie," he caressed Sondra's cheek, "we'll really weigh the matter."

Sondra had really expected an all-out no, so she was elated with the answer she received. Maybe she really would get to Israel. Over the past year she had realized that what Howie had said about their plan to find the Torah scroll had been the truth. It was a childish daydream, little more sophisticated than their grammar school plan of hopping freight trains and traveling across America. But realizing that the trip to Mafdner was not going to happen just made her desire to visit Israel all the stronger. Perhaps Howie would be interested in joining the group, too. She knew Aunt Irene and Uncle Herbert would agree to anything to get him away from Patty. She'd have to wait until he was in a good mood to talk to him about it. Maybe he really would be interested.

Chapter Sixteen

S ondra never got a chance to talk to Howie about the trip.

After school on Monday, she rode with him, in Aunt Irene's car, to the store. They talked about the University of Colorado the whole way there and once at Apple's, Uncle Simon sent her to the children's department and Howie to shoes. The rest of the week, Howie was preoccupied and rather irritable. Sondra hoped it was because of trouble with Patty, but suspected that it was on account of a term paper that was overdue. Maybe they'd be able to take a lunch break together Saturday.

The house was surprisingly quiet as Sondra made her way down the stairs early Saturday morning. There was no radio, no water running, no sound of boiled milk being poured into glass galleon jars. It was still dark out, but as Sondra walked through the living room, she was able to see her parents sitting at the kitchen table doing nothing. They looked at her as she entered the room and then gave each other a long look. Helga's eyes were swollen and she silently nodded at her husband.

"Sit down, sweetie," Julius ordered.

Sondra did as she was told, her heart beating rapidly.

Her father took her hands in his. "There was a bad accident late last night. Four kids were killed. One of them was Howie."

"I don't understand," Sondra's lower lip began to tremble as if her teeth were chattering but she was not cold. "Howie had to get up early to go to the store. He wouldn't have stayed out late."

"Well, he did," Helga didn't mean to snap.

Sondra studied her parents, trying to make some sense out of what they were telling her. She tried to keep her lip from shaking, but it would not stop. "Why didn't you wake me?"

"He was already gone," Julius shook his head.

"He died instantly," Helga added gently. "He didn't suffer."

Julius kept his daughter's hands in his and the three sat in silence.

"Who were the others?" Sondra finally asked.

Again her parents shared long looks.

Helga sighed and wrung her hands. "Patty, Charlie Carson…"

"And Joy," Sondra said resignedly.

"I'm sorry," Helga put her arms around her daughter. Sondra let her mother embrace her, but she did not cry. The tears were stuck in her throat and it ached horribly, but she could not cry.

Julius finally let go of Sondra's hands and stood up. "Your Oma should be awake now. I told Herbert I would break the news to her."

"I'll come with you," Helga stood up, also.

"You're going to leave me here by myself?" Sondra knew she sounded like a five-year-old, but she was afraid to be alone.

"Get dressed quickly," Helga answered. "You can come with us."

Later, when Sondra looked back on the day it was a blur of different memories with no beginning or end.

The front page of the morning paper would haunt her for years. Charlie's red Jaguar was a mangled mess, hit by a Santa Fe locomotive. Rescue workers were gathered around the scene. The midnight sky was dark and cloudy. It looked like something from a nightmare.

It had been a shock to see her Aunt Irene in her nightgown and robe without make-up or her hair brushed. Sondra wondered if her elegant aunt would ever care about her appearance again. Would her Uncle Herbert ever laugh again? Her Oma seemed to have aged ten years from the time her father had told her the news.

Sondra had finally been able to cry with Lisa. The two cousins had sat together on Lisa's bed and tried to make sense of the accident. Recalling all the times she had prayed that Howie would not marry Patty, Sondra had worried if this might have been God's answer to her prayers.

By midmorning, almost all of the family had gathered at Irene and Herbert's home. Everyone had something to say and there were countless calls to be made. Finding the phone always busy, numerous friends and acquaintances stopped by. The doorbell did not stop ringing. Conversations were going on in every corner of the house. Sondra's head was pounding and her eyes hurt. So when Jane came to the door to offer her sympathy and ask Sondra if she wanted to go for a walk, Sondra gratefully agreed.

Although it seemed light years earlier, it had been just a little over a week ago that she had told Brian all Jane wanted to talk about was Jesus. Sondra had spent most of the fall avoiding conversations with her old friend, but now she appreciated Jane's company. Silently and companionably, they headed for the university campus. There was no problem finding a vacant bench. The cold, dreary weather kept most of the students indoors, but it was perfect for Sondra's mood.

"Joy's funeral is going to be Monday afternoon," Jane broke the silence as they settled under a naked oak tree.

"Oh?"

"Are you going to come?"

"I don't know." Sondra dug her hands deeper into her coat pocket.

"I talked to Christine. She's coming in. She wants to see you. If you're not up to going, maybe we should get together afterwards, just the three of us."

"And talk about Joy." Sondra nodded. "That might be nice."

She sighed and tried to imagine sitting with her friends and having a nice time.

"When is Howie's funeral?"

"Tomorrow at one. His grandparents and some other relatives are flying into Wichita in the morning. I think my father and Oscar are going to pick them up."

"You know, when I heard the news I called your house and no one answered, so I got dressed and went to Apple's. Someone told me that none of the family came to work today."

"I forgot all about the store," Sondra answered diffidently. "It sure doesn't seem important right now."

There was another silence as Sondra watched two squirrels scamper between the trees.

"Sondra," Jane spoke earnestly, "I feel so terrible about Howie. If only he had accepted Jesus as his savior he would be in Heaven now, instead of burning in Hell. But it's not too late for you."

"Don't do this." Sondra shook her head. "Don't take advantage of my grief. God made me Jewish for a reason."

"I just want to help you because I care about you."

"No, Jane," Sondra moaned. "If you stop now we can still be friends. If you try and convert me now, there will be nothing left of our friendship."

"Have it your way," Jane raised her hands in submission and smiled graciously. Her eyes did not smile, though, and Sondra knew, even though they talked quietly on the way back to Howie's house, that their friendship was finished. Of course, everything she knew of her life in Lincoln High School was finished.

Even though the temperature was predicted to be only thirty-five degrees, the sun was shining the next day and that made it bearable at the cemetery. While there had been only a handful of people at both Opa's and Uncle Eli's funerals, there were so many people at Howie's that the crowd overflowed into the pasture. Since she was part of the family, Sondra was up close, next to the open grave, but she still saw many faces of her own and Howie's classmates in the crowd.

Everyone seemed to be in a state of shock, and suddenly Sondra realized that it was not only the Apfelbaum family that had been struck a blow, but also the Carsons, the Jenkinses, and the Charleses. And anyone who was connected to any of the four families would have a share in the grief. That meant about everyone in school, and probably most of the town, would be grieving. She knew that when she went back to school, she would be the center of attention, just as she had shared Howie's spotlight four years earlier when the write-up of his bar mitzvah had been in the Sunday paper. She did not know how she was going to face it.

Sondra did not go back to school right away. Following the funeral, as they all sat eating the dairy mourners' meal, Uncle Herbert announced that he was going to observe a full week of *shiva* for his son.

"Who is going to feed the cattle?" Berta asked.

"Mac can handle things for the week. If there are any problems he can call me. I'll be here." Herbert wiped his eyes with his handkerchief.

Sondra remembered that the family had sat shiva when Opa had died. But that had been erev Pesah, and they had only sat for an hour. Then they had gotten up and showered and begun the Seder. What a subdued Seder that had been. Sondra knew from her reading that the only ones who were supposed to sit shiva were Howie's parents and sister. As only a cousin, she was not even considered a mourner, but she certainly felt like a mourner. Her grandmother wasn't a mourner either, but Sondra was sure Oma would be at her son's house for the week. So would Aunt Irene's parents. Most likely Helga would spend most of the week there, too, helping out with the cooking and laundry. Sondra was certain that she did not belong in school the coming week. She should be at Howie's helping her mother. Right now Lisa and Rachel were inseparable, but Rachel was going back to Kansas City that evening and Lisa would need her. So would Oma, for that matter.

Later, after the house was cleaned up and kaddish recited at the evening service, Sondra told her parents what she wanted to do. To her surprise, they did not hesitate for even a moment to give her permission to stay out of school for the week.

Although there had been hundreds at Howie's funeral, few came to his home to pay a condolence call. Most people felt it was a Jewish custom and that they did not belong. But a few teachers, some of his teammates and the neighbors stopped by in the evenings. Dr. Cohen made sure to bring some Jewish students every evening for the services so that Herbert could say kaddish.

The mornings turned out to be family time. Sitting in the living room they looked at old pictures and shared stories about Howie. Sondra reminded them about the first time Howie had worked in the store and had gotten the price on the dress pants wrong and he had sold fifteen pairs of pants in two hours and Uncle Simon had lost money on every one of them. They laughed so hard at that story that they had tears in their eyes and then they cried.

"I wish it could have been me instead of Howie," Uncle Simon said sorrowfully. "I've had eighty-nine good years. He only had sixteen."

"That's not what God wanted," Irene answered gently.

Sondra noticed that her aunt was wearing her make-up and jewelry again. Next week, she would be going back to her volunteer work at the hospital. On the outside, it looked as if all was normal, but Sondra couldn't help but wonder if her aunt would ever be the same on the inside.

Lisa was very grateful for her cousin's company. They spent a lot of time in Lisa's room talking together, just the two of them. On Thursday, Lisa brought up the subject of God and questioned why He had let the accident happen.

"Remember how I told you I was jealous of Howie?" Lisa asked

"Yes." Sondra nodded her head.

"Do you think God is punishing me for being jealous?"

118

"No!" Sondra cried. She put her arm around her younger cousin. "All brothers and sisters are jealous of each other sometimes."

"I'll never be able to be jealous of him again," Lisa spoke mournfully.

"No," Sondra agreed. "And now we don't have to worry about him marrying Patty."

"Do you think that's why the accident happened?" Lisa asked.

"I don't know," Sondra answered miserably. "I used to pray every night that he wouldn't marry her, but this isn't the way I wanted God to answer me."

"Maybe God punished Howie for dating a non-Jew," Lisa stated. "What do you think?"

"I don't know," Sondra answered helplessly. All the wonderful Shabbats she had experienced had not prepared her for philosophical discussions about death. As she was searching for a comforting answer there was a knock on the door.

"Sondra," Helga called, "you have a visitor."

Tucking her blouse in, Sondra followed her mother into the living room and was surprised to see Mr. Marcus talking compassionately with her aunt and uncle and the others.

Chapter Seventeen

"Why did God punish my cousin?" Sondra asked Mr. Marcus as they walked the same path she and Jane had walked five days earlier.

"Sondra, I can't begin to pretend that I understand Hashem's ways," Mr. Marcus spoke slowly. "I can't even say for sure that your cousin was punished. Maybe it was a reward."

"What do you mean?" Waiting for an explanation, Sondra surveyed the campus looking for an empty bench. The weather was warmer and there were a number of students outside. Several stared at the older man with the black hat and beard, but no one said anything. Sondra spotted an empty bench near the entrance of the library.

"Back in the beginning of the Torah," Mr. Marcus sat down and turned to Sondra, "we learn that everyone lived for hundreds of years, right?"

Sondra nodded.

"One man, Hanoch, lived until only sixty-five years old. The Sages say that the reason he died so early was because, although he was a good man, he had the kind of nature that would cause him to go after the wrong crowd. At the age of sixty-five, he still had not committed any real sins and he would still be able to get his full share in *olam haba*..."

"What's that?"

"The World to Come. The afterlife."

"So we believe there is life after death?"

"Most definitely."

"How do we know for sure?"

Mr. Marcus smiled kindly. "Let me tell you a parable. There are two twins in their mother's womb. One thinks that there is more to the world than just swimming in prenatal fluid and the other is certain that there is nothing more to life. When the first brother is born, the second brother knows that he has lost his twin forever. In the midst of his mourning, however, he is plunged into the world and he sees how mistaken he really was. So it is for life after death."

Mr. Marcus watched the chattering students pass by as he let Sondra think over his allegory.

"Howie was killed in a car wreck on Shabbos with the non-Jewish girl he was dating. Do you think he's burning in hell now?"

"No, Sondra, no," Mr. Marcus shook his head. "Every Jew is guaranteed a share in olam haba. What he does with his life affects how big his share will be."

"You mean how many mitzvahs he does?"

"Yes."

"Howie did not do very many mitzvahs," Sondra shook her head sadly.

"I don't know about that," Mr. Marcus objected. "I saw him come write letters for Soviet Jews when he was in Kansas City. You told me how he used to help your grandmother at least once a week. He told me that he went to the monthly Shabbos services here. We have no way of knowing how Hashem keeps score of the mitzvahs we do. Your cousin did not keep Shabbos, that's true, but he had never seen the beauty of Shabbos. He cannot be held accountable for not doing what he did not know how to do."

"My friend told me that he's in hell because he did not believe in Jesus."

"That's ridiculous!" Mr. Marcus shook his hands impatiently. "That's not even worth wasting time discussing it."

"Okay," Sondra nodded. "So you're saying that every Jew gets to go to – what did you call it?"

"Olam haba."

"Olam haba. But why did that man from the beginning die so early?"

"Because if he was going to follow the bad crowd, then he would start doing sins, *aveirot*, that he knew he shouldn't do. That would make his portion in olam haba smaller and that would be a shame."

"Oh."

As Sondra was reasoning through what Mr. Marcus had just told her, one of the Jewish coeds came by.

"Hello, Sondra," she broke into Sondra's thoughts. "I'm so sorry to hear about your cousin. I was away for the weekend and did not make it to the funeral."

"Oh, thank you." Sondra hesitated for just a moment. "My aunt and uncle are sitting shiva if you want to stop by."

"Maybe I will," the coed said. "I'll tell some of the others. Thank you for telling me. Is this one of your relatives?"

"Excuse me. This is a friend, Mr. Marcus from Kansas City. This is Wendy Rosen."

"Pleased to meet you," the girl held out her hand.

"Nice to meet you, too," Mr. Marcus smiled charmingly. "I don't shake hands with women, though, so forgive me for not shaking yours."

"Okay," Wendy shrugged. Her face was puzzled, but not insulted. "How long are you in for?"

"Just the day. I thought Sondra might need someone to talk to."

"That's so nice!" the girl exclaimed. "I need to do some studying, so I'll see you later."

Sondra watched her walk up the steps and enter the library. Then she turned to Mr. Marcus.

"So Howie didn't lose his part in the World to Come for not keeping Shabbos because he did not know anything about keeping Shabbos. Right?"

Mr. Marcus nodded.

"So, if I know about Shabbos and don't keep it I will lose part of what I'm supposed to get, right?"

"Perhaps."

"Then I should start keeping Shabbos here in Lincoln."

"If you're able," Mr. Marcus answered gently.

"I guess I'm going to have to try." Sondra spoke with determination.

"Any time you need help or have questions you can call me. You can even call collect."

"Thank you," Sondra whispered and wiped away the tears that were falling down her face.

Chapter Eighteen

"Welcome back, Sondra," Mrs. Wiggs gave Sondra's shoulder a gentle squeeze. "I'm glad you're here. We're having tryouts this afternoon."

Sondra smiled weakly as she sat in her place.

The next day Mrs. Wiggs stopped Sondra as she was leaving the classroom.

"Where were you yesterday?"

Sondra felt her face flushing and, even though she had rehearsed what she was going to say to the drama teacher over and over again, she found herself stammering.

"I've decided not to be in any more plays. You see, well, I want to observe my Sabbath right, and going to practices or, uh, performances on Friday nights would be, well, kind of problematic."

"I see," Mrs. Wiggs nodded. "I won't pretend I'm not disappointed. Maybe you can help us out with some of the backstage work on the weekdays."

Sondra nodded and Mrs. Wiggs did not seem to notice that it was only halfheartedly. If only Uncle Simon could have been as understanding as her teacher. As Sondra walked to her next class she went over in her mind the conversation she had had with her great-uncle. Despite the week of shiva she had gone to the store Thursday evening, the night that all the stores stayed open late.

Fifteen minutes before closing she had approached her uncle in his office upstairs.

Dignified as ever in his three-piece suit, Simon Apfelbaum was busy signing payroll checks. Sondra tried to remember all the Hershey chocolate bars and silver dollars he had given her as a child, but all she could think of now was that he thought he was in charge of all the relatives.

"Yes, Sondra, how are you feeling?"

"Okay," Sondra sighed and wound her ring around her finger, "only I wanted to tell you that I'm not going to be able to work Saturday."

Simon put his pen down and stared at his great-niece.

"Sondra, we all know how badly you feel about losing Howie, but he was not your brother. I've been understanding all week, but I need you Saturday."

"I'm sorry, Uncle Simon," Sondra took a deep breath. "I decided today to keep Shabbos. I know I should have given you two weeks' notice." Seeing her uncle's face turning red Sondra spoke quickly. "I will ask a friend from school to work in my place. I will bring her in tomorrow and show her what to do. You don't have to pay me."

"I know I don't have to pay you!" Uncle Simon roared. "If it wasn't for me you wouldn't be alive, you ungrateful..." With great effort her uncle closed his mouth and swallowed back his angry words.

"I know it was because of you that my father was able to get into America," Sondra could not believe how calmly she was talking. "I am very grateful, but I have to do what I think is right. And I think keeping Shabbos is the right thing to do, at least for me."

Uncle Simon shook his head. His eyes were still angry. "This is 1970 and you want to live like you're in the Middle Ages?"

"Yes."

"I will be patient with you, Sondra. I know that you have been through quite a trauma. But you are taking this Jewish thing too far. Your cousin Bernice is a fine Jew and she worked for me for years."

Sondra took a deep breath. "I'm sorry, Uncle Simon, but I am not Bernice."

"Well, you could learn a lot from her. Your job here will always be available for you, as soon as you come to your senses and decide you're willing to work on Saturdays."

As soon as Julius saw his daughter's face, he knew something was wrong and on the short ride home Sondra repeated the whole, sorry conversation.

"I see," Julius said as they entered the kitchen. "You made a big decision today."

"What?" Helga had just returned home from the shiva house minutes before them.

Quickly, as he poured himself a cup of coffee, Julius explained what had happened.

"You feel very strongly about this Shabbos thing?" Helga asked. The three of them sat around the kitchen table.

Sondra just nodded.

"You don't think you could just work until the holiday season is over and then start keeping Shabbos?"

Sondra shook her head. "I told Uncle Simon I'd find someone to work in my place, and I will."

Julius rubbed his eyes and forehead. "I must say, Sondra, you sure sound determined."

"Do you mind?"

"Is this what that Mr. Marcus told you to do?" Helga answered Sondra's question with a question of her own.

"No, he just answered a lot of my questions and the answers made me decide to do this. Do you mind?" Sondra repeated.

Neither of her parents answered immediately.

"What are you going to do differently than you did before?" Helga finally asked.

"I'm not going to drive to the services anymore."

Sondra's parents nodded their heads. They had expected that.

"I won't answer the phone, even if I'm the only one in the house. And if there's a call for me, I won't come to the phone."

Again her parents nodded and looked at her expectantly.

Sondra took a breath and plunged on. Mr. Marcus had warned her that her parents might be hostile to or supportive of her desire to keep Shabbat. A lot would depend on how she presented it.

"I would like to tape some lights on so no one will turn them off, like in the bathroom and the kitchen. Would that be okay?"

"I think we can put up with that," Julius answered.

"I'd also like to unscrew the light in the fridge and freezer so I can open them on Shabbos. Can I?"

"As long as it doesn't hurt them," Helga said.

"It shouldn't. Debbie's mother does it every week."

"What else?" Julius asked.

Sondra shrugged her shoulder helplessly. "That's all I can think of now."

"Are you going to eat with us?" Helga asked.

"Oh, well," Sondra thought for a minute. "In the winter, Friday night won't be a problem. In the summer, it may be too early for me to eat. And during the day, at noon time, I can sit with you, but I'll only eat cold food."

Helga nodded her head, feeling that she could handle what Sondra had explained.

"That sounds okay," Julius said, "but I don't want you trying to change your mother or me. Is that understood?"

Sondra nodded, glad to have her parent's approval.

By Friday morning all the family knew about Sondra's decision. Berta thought the girl had gone mad because of Howie's death. Oscar, as always, thought whatever Sondra did was fine, even if her absence would make more work for him. Frayda just nodded her head. She had not said much ever since Julius had told her about her grandson's death. Uncle Herbert did not say anything either, but he thought to himself how different Howie's life would have been if it had been he who had decided to keep Shabbat. Despite her grief, Aunt Irene told Sondra that she was proud of her for standing up for what she believed.

The hardest part for Sondra during her first week back at school was deciding where to eat her lunch. There would be no Joy and no Howie to sit with. She supposed she should sit with some of the drama crowd, but after she had not shown up at the tryouts she was not sure that she was welcome. She did not realize it, but Lisa was struggling with the same problem.

"Do you want to eat lunch with me?" Lisa asked when they happened to meet at the cafeteria door.

"Sure." Sondra knew she should be embarrassed to be seen sitting with a freshman, but under the circumstances she wasn't.

"No one knows what to say to me," Lisa said ruefully as she pushed her tray through the line. "So no one is saying anything."

"I know," Sondra was sympathetic. She paid for her iced tea and followed her cousin to a table in the corner.

Lisa waited for Sondra to finish saying the blessing on her sandwich. "Don't you think it's going to be hard to pack a lunch for school every day?"

"Maybe, but I'm determined to do this right."

"Do what?"

"Keep kosher and Shabbos."

"That's what that man from Kansas City told you to do?"

"No," Sondra shook her head and repeated what she had told her parents. "He didn't tell me to do anything. He just answered a lot of questions and I decided now was the time to try to do what I've been wanting to do for almost a year now."

Even after Lisa's friends relaxed and began to talk to her like a normal person, she still liked sitting with Sondra in the lunchroom. She used the time to ask questions about Judaism or talk about Howie. Sondra worked hard in school, but spent little time socializing. Mrs. Wiggs gave up asking her to stop by rehearsals to help out. And most of her classmates stopped offering her rides home. That was fine with Sondra. She did not mind the walk home and usually stopped in for a short visit with her grandmother on the way.

In the beginning it was hard to get a conversation started with Frayda. She seemed preoccupied and didn't really concentrate on anything Sondra said. She had stopped baking and her handiwork lay untouched. Still, Sondra did not give up and finally got Frayda to agree to teach her how to crochet a yarmulke. With the crochet hook in hand Frayda relaxed, and once again she began to tell Sondra stories of the family.

Reading and homework took up most of Sondra's evenings and afternoons. Every so often a couple of the Jewish freshmen from the university would call her and invite her to join them in activities at Lincoln State. Even though their interest in anything Jewish was minimal, Sondra felt more comfortable with them than she did with her old high school friends. And, of course, she lived for her monthly Shabbats in Kansas City. It was after Passover that she made her decision.

"Mother, Daddy," she announced at the dinner table, "I've decided not to go to the University of Colorado. I'm going to stay here and study at Lincoln State."

Both Julius and his wife put down their soupspoons and stared at their daughter.

"Do you think you can get accepted?" Helga finally asked.

"I already was."

Julius and Helga exchanged long looks. It was Julius who spoke.

"Punishing yourself is not going to do anything to help Howie. He's gone and we all have to go on with our lives."

"You don't understand," Sondra shook her head. "It has nothing to do with punishing myself or helping Howie. It's Oma and Lisa I'm thinking about."

The ticking of the German grandfather clock seemed unusually loud as Sondra's parents studied her face.

"You need to think about yourself," Helga said. "What kind of life are you going to have here? What are you going to do when you want to have fun? Go to the lake with your Oma? What about Shabbos? You're going celebrate it like a hermit and ruin your eyes with all your reading."

"I've done some nice things with the girls from college," Sondra spoke softly, but she was determined. "Lisa is just three years younger than I am and she can be company for me, too. And as for Shabbos," Sondra gave a nervous little laugh, "with the money that we're saving on in-state tuition I thought I could buy a used car and drive to Kansas City for the weekends."

Again her parents exchanged long looks.

"We'll have to discuss that," Julius said.

Chapter Nineteen

*I*n Lincoln no one had any objections to Sondra's change of plans. The same could not be said for her family and friends in the rest of the country. It seemed that almost every day there was another cross letter waiting for Sondra in the metal mailbox on the road. Bernice wrote her that she was a fool. Aunt Lotte told her she was making a mistake. Debbie begged her to change her mind. And Brian was angry with her. She ignored Brian's anger and wrote back that she had almost finished the yarmulke she was crocheting for him. He ignored her letter, but did write her a thank you note for the yarmulke.

Debbie spent all of Shavuot trying to talk Sondra into going to Stern College with her. Julius and Helga had decided to buy a used car for Sondra as a graduation present, but Debbie was not impressed with Sondra's plans to come to Kansas City for most Shabbats.

"I won't be here. Marc won't be here. The twins won't be here. Who are you going to spend Shabbos with?"

"Miriam is still here."

"For one more year. And then what?"

"I'll cross that bridge when I get there," Sondra sighed. "I have to do this, Debbie. Try to understand."

"I guess I really can't understand what you're going through," Debbie echoed Sondra's sigh. "I can't imagine what it was like losing your cousin. I guess if I'm a good friend I should be more supportive."

"I hope you'll keep writing to me." Sondra ignored the reference to Howie.

"Of course."

"I'll be at the Marcuses a lot for Shabbos."

"Really?" Debbie raised her eyebrows. "Mrs. Marcus doesn't mind?"

"I don't think so. She said there was a lot she could teach me about Shabbos when I help her in the kitchen."

"That sounds interesting," Debbie conceded.

Debbie did not realize how close that weekend in Kansas City came to making Sondra change her mind. Hearing everyone's exciting plans for the next year made Sondra feel left out and, for the first time in Kansas City, different. During the long bus ride home Sondra had almost decided to call the University of Colorado to ask if she could be accepted again.

As soon as she arrived in Lincoln, though, before she could even broach the subject, her parents began talking about graduation.

"I really don't want to go," Sondra complained. "It's going to be hot and crowded and impersonal."

"Well, if that isn't one of the most selfish things I ever heard!" Helga exclaimed.

"What?" Sondra cried out, stung by the criticism. After all, she was being selfless by giving up the University of Colorado to keep up her grandmother's spirits and look out for Lisa.

Her father cleared his throat. "What your mother is trying to say is that we have been looking forward for years to seeing our daughter graduate."

"I didn't think about that," Sondra mumbled.

"We were planning to have a family party at the house afterwards, if," Helga added sarcastically, "that wouldn't put you out too much."

"No, Mom," Sondra swallowed the lump in her throat. "That would be fine."

Sondra tried not to resent her mother. For over a year they had not had any real blowups. Why couldn't her mother understand how difficult the graduation ceremony was going to be for her? Pleading exhaustion, she went up to her room as soon as they arrived at the farm. In the morning Helga was busy straining milk and Sondra was running late, so she said a quick goodbye to her mother, avoiding any unpleasantness. She did not know what would be waiting for her when she got back later that afternoon.

So it was without enthusiasm that Sondra left school Tuesday afternoon. Just as she was turning onto Main Street a light blue Oldsmobile pulled up next to her and honked. Aunt Irene rolled down the automatic window on the passenger side.

"How about a ride?"

"Sure," Sondra scrambled in, appreciating the car's air conditioning. As she fastened her seat belt, she studied her aunt. Howie's death had not changed Irene's elegant appearance. Although she had cut her honey-blonde hair several years earlier, her hairstyle was as fashionable as ever. She had just the right amount of makeup and jewelry, but there were definite wrinkles around her eyes and forehead.

"How about stopping for a cold drink before you go to your Oma's?"

"Okay," Sondra gave her aunt a questioning look.

"I wanted to catch you already back at school, but I was late leaving the hospital."

"Oh."

The four o'clock news came on and Sondra was quiet as Irene found a parking place in front of Molly's, the old drugstore downtown.

"I talked to your mother today," Irene went straight to the point as soon as they had settled themselves in the red, vinyl booth. "She told me there's tension between you all about graduation."

Sondra just nodded.

"I imagine that going to graduation without Howie is going to be very hard for you."

"Yes," Sondra nodded, surprised to hear her aunt say her son's name so easily.

"That's part of it."

"And since you are no longer participating in any of the plays, you really don't feel part of the class."

"That's for sure." Sondra played with the saltshaker.

"I understand," Irene smiled. "On the other hand, your parents never had a high school graduation. Your father took English at the high school here, but he never graduated. And your mother never went to high school. She got her diploma by correspondence course. I was always so proud of her." Irene took a tissue out of her purse and blew her nose.

"I'm proud of her, too," Sondra protested.

"I know you are," Irene answered hastily. "I just want you to understand where your mother is coming from. She enjoyed so much seeing you happy in school, doing well, with some good friends, and being part of the drama department. It was almost as if she was reliving her lost youth through you."

"Okay," Sondra sighed. "So by seeing me graduate it's going to be like my mother is graduating."

"Something like that."

"But she's graduating the week after from the university with a Ph.D.!"

Irene shook her head. "It's not the same thing."

"So, I'll go to the graduation." Sondra said in a flat voice.

"Thank you, Sondra."

"What for?"

"For being so mature and understanding. For caring about Lisa. For wanting to look out for your Oma."

"Do you think I'm doing the right thing, going to Lincoln State?"

Irene took a long sip of her DietRite. "I don't know if it's the right thing for you. I really don't. But I know it is a good thing for this family."

Irene's wrinkles deepened. She was worried. She had been worried ever since Howie had become so serious about his girl-friend. She was afraid that she and Herbert might start blaming each other. That had not happened, but now she was scared that they would start blaming each other for letting Howie go out that horrible night. She knew the statistics about the high divorce rates after couples had lost a child. She did not want anything to happen to her marriage. She prayed that she and Herbert would grow even closer, but she was frightened. And she was worried about Lisa. What path would the girl take? Would she follow her brother or Sondra? Getting her to go to Kansas City should not be hard. Lisa was always dying to visit Rachel. But Lotte said that Rachel was not interested in the youth group. Rather, she was planning to try out for cheerleading the next year. Irene looked upon Sondra as her hope.

"Another thing, about graduation," Irene gazed steadily at her niece. "There's going to be a memorial for Howie and the others. I think you will want to be there for that."

"You're probably right," Sondra conceded.

When she came home from Oma's an hour later Helga was at the kitchen sink, cheerfully washing out glass jars.

"Hi, honey, did you have a good day?"

"Yes," Sondra nodded and gave her mother a kiss. "How about you?"

"Fine. I got a letter from Lotte. She said they are planning to come down for the graduation." Helga spoke shyly. Although Irene had called while Sondra was at Frayda's, Helga was still not sure what kind of reception her statement would receive. She needn't have worried.

"It will be great to see them," Sondra smiled. "Hey, maybe Debbie can come with them."

"Maybe," Helga nodded. "Write Aunt Lotte and ask if they can squeeze her in."

That was the whole conversation about Sondra's decision to go to the graduation. No mention of how different it would have been if Howie were still there. No recognition of how hard it would be for Sondra. No acknowledgement that her life had been totally turned upside down.

The next evening, though, after Julius had finished milking, Aunt Irene and Uncle Herbert stopped by with a big, gift-wrapped box. Julius and Helga ushered them into the living room as if they had been expecting them and called Sondra in from the kitchen.

"Hi, sweetie," Herbert greeted his niece with a kiss.

"We brought you your graduation present a little early," Irene patted the spot next to her on the couch.

"Thank you." Sondra carefully began to peel back the scotch tape so the paper could be used again.

The four adults waited impatiently for her to discover the beautiful, brocade suitcase.

"Thank you," Sondra said uncertainly.

"There's a smaller one inside that one," Herbert announced.

"Okay," Sondra felt her cheeks flush as she unzipped the large suitcase. What in the world did she need luggage for if she was staying at Lincoln State?

As if reading her thoughts her father cleared his throat. "Your mother and I have a present for you, too."

"I thought you were buying me the Nova."

"We're using the money we're saving on not paying out-of-state tuition for that," Helga answered. "That's not a graduation present."

Julius looked lovingly at his daughter. "We're sending you to Israel for a month for a graduation present."

"What?"

"We did discuss it on the way home from Kansas City, just like we said we would," Helga told Sondra. "And we decided that if you were going to be in Colorado for almost the whole year we did not want to send you away for the summer. Then," Helga sighed and glanced apologetically at Irene, "everything changed."

"We contacted the Federation and there was still room on their program," Julius said. "They said there were only two kids from Kansas City going. You'll be the third."

"What about my job?"

"I spoke to them and told them you wouldn't be able to start until after the fifth of July," Helga explained. "I hope you're pleased with our surprise?" she asked anxiously.

Remembering how she had once planned on trying to talk Howie into going with her, Sondra could only nod her head. Tears poured silently down her cheeks, but she was smiling.

Chapter Twenty

*F*rom the quick swerve and loud honk, Sondra realized that the bus driver had narrowly missed hitting an old Arab leading a donkey across the busy street. She shook her head in disbelief. In the last hour since she had left Lod Airport she had seen enough strange sights to last a lifetime: soldiers with machine guns slung casually over their soldiers, Arab women walking with bulging baskets on their heads, religious men dressed all in black from their heads to their feet, rusty trucks at the roadside with memorial signs next to them, and more.

"Is it what you expected?" Robin, her seatmate, asked her.

"I didn't know what to expect. I'm just glad I'm here," Sondra squeezed her hands in excitement. "What about you?"

"My sister came on this tour last year. She told me everything."

With a squeal of the brakes the bus stopped and Ilana, one of the group's leaders, stood up with the microphone.

"We are going to make one stop before we go to the hostel. Your belongings will be safe, but please put on your hats. Everyone follow me."

"All I want to do is go to sleep," Robin complained.

As exhausted as she was, Sondra did *not* want to go to sleep. She wanted to see everything. As she left the bus, she joined the two girls from Kansas City. They were from the big Reform

Temple and Sondra had never met them before, but they were friendly. All of the thirty-eight kids on the tour were friendly, but all of them were from big cities. They looked at Sondra almost as if she were a creature from another planet when they found out that she lived on a farm.

When they all met at JFK airport in New York, Sondra had been surprised to see that none of the boys were wearing yarmulkes. And when a group of men with black hats approached the boys to put on *tefillin* – the leather straps and black boxes that religious men don daily in order to pray each morning – only two agreed. The tour was supposed to be strictly kosher, but Sondra wondered if she was the only one who cared. She did not have time to worry about that now, though. Ilana and Itzhak, the other leader, were racing through a crowded, dark marketplace and down a narrow alley. If she didn't pay attention, Sondra knew she would be lost. Almost running she descended some stairs, made a few turns, and then came to an open plaza full of sunlight. There, in front of her, stood the Western Wall, just like it looked in all the pictures. Emotions from the past seven months caught up with her. She burst into tears.

No one from the group noticed Sondra fumbling in her bag for tissues. An older, wrinkled woman with a white kerchief covering her graying hair stopped at Sondra's side.

"Why are you crying?" she asked kindly in heavily accented English as she handed Sondra a clean handkerchief.

"I… I don't know," Sondra wiped her eyes. "I wanted to come here for so long."

"And now that you are here you are going to stay?"

Sondra shook her head slowly. "No, my parents won't let me stay. They're waiting for me to come home."

"This is your home," the woman said. "When you go back to America, remember that. This is home for every Jew."

"Sondra, are you okay?"

Without meaning to, Sondra turned her back on the woman and saw Robin waving to her. She waved in return and when she turned around to thank the woman and return the handkerchief, the woman had disappeared.

"Who was that?"

"I don't know."

"Come." Robin took Sondra by the arm. "Let's go to the Wall. We're supposed to write a note and put it in between the cracks."

Once again, Sondra wished that Debbie had come with her on the trip. She knew the cantor's daughter would have directed her to pray at the Wall and not just make a wish.

The next three days were a whirl of touring Jerusalem. They saw museums, tombs, and many different neighborhoods of the city. In between they went swimming, planted trees, and went to a sound and light show. Before she knew it, it was Friday afternoon and Sondra asked Ilana what they would be doing for Shabbat.

"Tomorrow's a free day," the young woman spoke offhandedly. "What do you want to do?"

"I want to have Shabbos," Sondra answered simply.

"Okay, that's cool. There are several *batei knesset* near the hostel."

"Several what?"

"Synagogues," Ilana translated somewhat impatiently. "Tomorrow you can have lunch anytime between eleven and one. That will give you plenty of time to even go to the Kotel if you want. There will be supper in the evening before Shabbos is over."

"Is the food going to be cooked on Shabbos?" Sondra asked nervously.

"Of course not," Ilana looked at Sondra as if she were an idiot.

Before sundown, the manager of the hostel directed Sondra and most of the other girls to light the Shabbat candles on a special table in the dining room. Itzhak escorted about half of the group to a local shul. Although she had never gone to Friday evening services in Kansas City, Sondra found she was able to follow the service. Afterwards people greeted them with "Shabbat shalom" and asked them where they were from. Someone had a cousin in Brooklyn and wanted to know if they knew him. On the way back to the hostel, they saw several other groups staying at the same place, coming back from different synagogues. There was indeed the spirit of Shabbat as they sat down in the dining hall and had a real Shabbat meal.

After the meal, however, Itzhak announced that whoever wanted to go with him to a private party at the Hebrew University campus should meet at the entrance of the hostel at ten o'clock. They should bring money for the Arab taxi. Sondra was disappointed to see how many wanted to go. She noticed, across the room, though, a group of French girls who were still sitting at their table and quietly singing Shabbat songs. Sondra decided to join them.

She did not know French, but several of the girls knew English and made her feel welcome. As she sang, Sondra looked the other girls over carefully. All were wearing long skirts, long sleeves, and nylon stockings. She felt rather self-conscious in her short-sleeved dress in which she had always felt comfortable in Kansas City. No one seemed to notice, though. After the French girls finished saying grace after meals, they invited Sondra to walk with them to the Western Wall the following morning. She eagerly accepted the invitation.

"I guess Shabbos is Shabbos in any language," Sondra said to herself as she walked to her room.

On Sunday morning, Ilana and Itzhak began banging on their group's doors before six o'clock. There was lots of moaning and complaining, but the two leaders did not care.

"The bus is leaving at seven. You need to have your bags in the lobby before breakfast. Let's go!"

"And I want three guys to help me load the bus!" Itzhak commanded.

Sondra was one of the first downstairs. She wanted to say goodbye to the French girls who were supposed to be flying back to France that evening, but not one of them entered the dining hall. At five to seven Sondra left, boarded the bus and sat down in the aisle seat that one of the girls had saved for her.

After a week together, everyone in the group had relaxed and become comfortable with one another. They went touring in the north of the country and in the south. Sometimes they traveled in air-conditioned buses, but more often than not, they rode in the backs of trucks. They went hiking in nature preserves, visited archeological sites, swam in the ocean, and saw the towns. Sondra quickly learned to cover herself with suntan lotion and fill her canteen with cold water every morning. She also learned to take the teasing about being a farmer's daughter in her stride.

They ate a big Israeli breakfast every morning and most days had full, meat meals both at noon and in the evening. During the last week, though, they began to see fish over and over, and some of the kids began complaining.

"Sorry," Ilana said most unsympathetically. "You're on a kosher tour and a lot of the places don't serve meat during the Nine Days."

"Nine days of what?" someone challenged.

"The nine days before Tisha b'Av." Although not especially observant, Ilana had come from a traditional home and she explained the days of mourning for the Beit Hamikdash that had been destroyed two thousand years earlier.

"When's Tisha b'Av?" Sondra asked nervously.

"Actually, it's on Shabbat" Ilana answered. "No one fasts on Shabbat, though. It's pushed off until Sunday."

Sondra kicked herself mentally. She vaguely remembered Debbie's explanation from last summer, but she had not learned any more about it. Should she fast? Why hadn't anyone told her Tisha b'Av was coming up? She couldn't call Mr. Marcus collect from Israel, but she really did not know what to do. She was on her own. This Shabbat was a free Shabbat. It had been planned weeks ago that she would go to Aunt Irene's cousin who lived on a religious kibbutz near the Jordanian border. She wouldn't have to be back with the group until Sunday night in Tel Aviv.

Chapter Twenty-One

The two previous Shabbatot had been spent similarly to that first Shabbat in Jerusalem. The group stayed at a hotel where those who wanted to observe a Shabbat of sorts could do so. The others were able to take advantage of Arab taxis and see the nightlife, go swimming, or shop for souvenirs. Shabbat on the kibbutz was a whole new experience.

Right before candle-lighting, the gate to the kibbutz was closed. All cars stopped. Radios were turned off. Almost everyone in the kibbutz headed to the synagogue that was located in the center of the settlement. Around the shul was a park with the greenest grass Sondra had ever seen. Young mothers sat on benches watching their children play. A few men with machine guns over their shoulders and prayer books in their hands did guard duty while they prayed. As the sun was setting Sondra felt a sense of peace, that Shabbat could almost be touched.

Aunt Irene's cousin, Leah, took Sondra to shul with her and after services were over introduced her to a number of her friends. To Sondra's delight, most of the founding members of the kibbutz were from Germany and Sondra was able to communicate in German.

"Do you think anyone here knew my mother or father in Germany?" Sondra asked Leah as they strolled from the synagogue to the dining hall.

"Mafdner?" Leah shook her head. "I don't think so. But my friend Shulamit grew up in Jesburg, not far from there. I'll introduce you."

Even though the plates on the tables in the dining hall were made of the cheap plastic that Sondra had seen all over Israel that summer, the white tablecloths and vases of flowers gave the hall a Shabbat atmosphere. Leah guided Sondra to her family's table and they sat down with Leah's husband and their three teenagers. The noise of one hundred and fifty men all making Kiddush at the same time was overwhelming, but then, after everyone had made the blessing over bread and the soup was served, there was complete quiet for a few minutes as they all began their Shabbat meal.

"How much longer are you going to be in Israel?" Rivka, Leah's daughter, asked politely.

"I'm leaving Monday evening," Sondra sighed.

With a few more questions, Sondra told them about all the places she had seen. Feeling comfortable, she finally asked about Tisha b'Av.

Leah's husband gave her a quick rundown of the laws of the three weeks, the nine days, and of Tisha b'Av itself.

"Is it important to fast?" Sondra asked.

"As important as Yom Kippur. The fast starts tomorrow night. We'll eat an early afternoon meal. Where are you planning on spending the fast?"

"I don't know," Sondra hesitated. "It's a free day. Some of the kids are planning to go to the Arab market and buy presents to take home, but if I'm fasting, I don't think it's a good idea."

"It's also inappropriate for the day."

"You're welcome to stay here," Leah said graciously. "We'll have a nice break-the-fast right after sundown."

"Or," her husband suggested, "you can go to my sister in Jerusalem. That way you can go to the Kotel, which is very appropriate for the day."

"That's what I'm doing," Rivka said. "You can come with me."

"Okay," Sondra smiled. Getting a bus from Jerusalem to Tel Aviv on Sunday night would not be a problem.

The meal finished quickly without any Shabbat songs and no dessert. Leah explained that everyone wanted to go back to their own homes and eat their own cakes.

It wasn't until after lunch the next day that Sondra met Shulamit.

"Jesburg is only forty kilometers from Mafdner," the older woman explained. "But by horse and wagon that was a long way. I do remember going there once for a "giving the Torah party." I was just a little girl and families from all over the area came. It made a big impression on me. Everyone so happy and dancing in honor of the Sefer Torah."

"I wonder whether it was our Sefer Torah?" Sondra could not help but exclaim.

"Your Sefer Torah?"

Playing with her ring, Sondra explained the story of the two Torah scrolls while the woman listened, fascinated.

"Obviously, it was one of them." She shook her head thoughtfully. "That celebration made such an impression on me. I think that's one of the reasons I stayed religious even after all the Nazis did to us."

"Did you...?" Sondra asked timidly, not wanting to interrupt the woman's thoughts, but anxious to ask her question. "Did you ever hear about what happened to Adolf Klein?"

"Adolf Klein," Shulamit thought for a few minutes. "The name sounds familiar, but then there are a lot of Kleins."

"That's true," Sondra agreed. Howie had said their idea was just a childish plan, but here, just by chance, she had met someone who had seen the Sefer Torah.

Rivka's Aunt Irma lived in a small apartment in Kiryat Moshe, a religious neighborhood a few minutes away from the central bus station. She made Sondra feel as comfortable as her niece, but she did not smile once.

"It's because of the day," Rivka explained on the way to the Kotel. "Normally my aunt is laughing and singing all the time."

Sondra had a hard time following the services that morning. She sat on the ground like everyone else, but understood little of what was going on around her. There were a number of women crying as if their hearts were broken. They seemed so strange and Sondra wondered how Mrs. Marcus or Debbie's mother would act if they were there. She followed Rivka's lead and did not sit in the bus on the way home. The afternoon dragged on and on as if it would never end, but finally it grew dark. Rivka's uncle and cousin came home from shul and they sat down to eat.

Although the mood was still somber, Sondra felt it was suitable to ask Rivka's uncle if he had grown up very near Mafdner.

"Actually, I'm from Frankfort, but my mother had a cousin who lived in Mafdner."

"Who?" Sondra felt her heart racing.

"Gerta Schuster."

"Is she in Israel, too?"

The man shook his head sadly. "She didn't make it out of the camps."

"I'm sorry." Sondra's eyes filled with tears.

"It's okay." Irma patted Sondra's hand. "It was a natural question."

Sondra nodded. "My Uncle Eli and Aunt Sopha Apfelbaum lived in Frankfort. Maybe you knew them?" she asked hopefully.

"Eli Apfelbaum? He had two children, a boy and a girl?"

Sondra nodded eagerly.

"Alfred Apfelbaum was a year ahead of me in school. We went to the same shul. How is he?"

Now it was Sondra's turn to shake her head sadly. "He was killed in the army."

"I'm so sorry."

"But Berta is fine," Sondra said quickly. "Her daughter, Bernice, is married and has an adorable little girl."

"Isn't that something!"

Both Rivka and Sondra offered to help clean up, but Irma shooed them away. "You get yourselves to the bus station. You both have a long ride ahead of you tonight."

To Sondra's delight she met five of the kids from the group as she boarded the bus to Tel Aviv. They sat together and talked about how they couldn't believe the trip was almost over and what they were looking forward to when they got home.

"I'm going straight to McDonald's as soon as I get off the plane," one girl declared.

"I wrote my mother to have plenty of root beer in the refrigerator when I get home."

"I can't wait to have normal toilet paper and tissues," Robin sighed.

"What about you, Sondra?" one of the boys teased. "Are you looking forward to getting home and milking the cows?"

"Can't wait."

"Don't be surprised if we show up at your door one day and demand some fresh milk," Robin said half-seriously.

"You're always welcome," Sondra answered, completely serious.

Later in bed, trying to fall asleep, Sondra thought over what was waiting for her at home. It would be good to see her parents, of course. And the rest of the family. She had presents for all of them that she would give out at Uncle Simon's birthday party. The old man had apparently forgiven her for refusing to work on Shabbat. His graduation gift to her had been a generous check that she had used to buy the presents.

Her car would be waiting for her and she looked forward to going to Kansas City for the weekends. She wondered if Brian was still upset with her. She knew that Debbie, at least, would be happy to see her. She had her job at the library waiting for her, and her grandmother and Lisa to look out for. Yes, she decided as she shut her eyes, it would be good to go home.

Chapter Twenty-Two

*B*y the time she reached the farmhouse late Tuesday, Sondra was so exhausted that she could barely converse.

"Go to sleep." Helga swallowed her disappointment. "We'll talk tomorrow."

"Are you sure?" Sondra knew her parents had been looking forward to her homecoming and hearing all about her trip.

"I'm sure."

"Sleep as late as you can," Julius added.

It was after noon when Sondra finally woke up the next day. By the time she finished dressing, her parents were all ready to leave for Uncle Simon's. The party was called for one o'clock and they would be the last ones there. As they drove up, Sondra saw Lisa and Rachel on the front porch, looking as if they were watching for her.

"I missed you," Lisa exclaimed. She and Sondra hugged each other. Sondra kissed Rachel and turned her attention back to Lisa.

"You look different."

Lisa smiled broadly.

"It's your nose," Sondra cried. "Did you have a nose job?"

Lisa nodded. "What do you think?"

Sondra studied her cousin. A smaller nose had softened Lisa's features. She looked less like Howie and far more feminine.

"You look lovely."

"She's going to have her pick of dates when school starts," Rachel predicted.

Sondra refrained from saying what she thought about Lisa dating.

"Hi, Sondra." Joey was the first one to greet her inside the house. "Did you have a good time in Israel?"

"Great, and I brought you back an army hat."

"Neat!"

Joey entered the living room at Sondra's side. She greeted Uncle Simon first. It was his ninetieth birthday and he had a full house. His grandson, Richard, had flown in, of course, as had Bernice, Robert, and their baby. Brenda and her husband had brought Uncle Nathan. Lotte and her family had come for the day. The Cohens and several other families from the university were there. And old-time employees kept stopping by to offer their congratulations.

Sondra quickly became the center of attention. Richard was the only other one who had visited Israel, but his last trip had been two years earlier. He was full of questions and everyone seemed interested in hearing the answers. Aunt Irene wanted to know all about her cousin. Sondra described the kibbutz and then told them about Leah's brother-in-law who knew Alfred.

"I remember the name," Berta spoke up. "I'm glad to know he survived the war and has a nice family." Embarrassed, she wiped a tear from her cheek.

"What was your favorite place?" Brenda asked.

"That's hard." Sondra was thoughtful. "The Kotel – the Western Wall – was really special. If I were going to live there, though, I think I would like to live in Safed."

"I hope you're *not* going to live there," Frayda said and everyone laughed.

Sondra stood up and went to her grandmother's side. "Don't worry, Oma. I have to finish college before I think about moving anywhere."

"Moving to Israel is not the worst thing you could do," Oscar said.

Sondra enjoyed the afternoon. The next day she began working at the university library. On Friday afternoon she threw her overnight bag in the back seat of the Nova, picked up Lisa, and the two of them set off for Kansas City.

"Are you sure you don't want to go with me to Debbie's?" Sondra asked as they pulled off the turnpike.

Lisa nodded emphatically. "Rachel has a new record I want to hear. We'll go to the cookout with you Saturday night."

"Okay," Sondra sighed.

It was good to see Debbie again. Her parents welcomed Sondra warmly. On Shabbat morning Sondra saw Brian in shul. He greeted Sondra at the kiddush, but it was not a warm greeting. Evidently he still had not forgiven her for backing out of going to the University of Colorado. Sondra tried to be philosophical about it as she walked home, listening to a chattering Debbie. Better to know that Brian could pout and hold a grudge now instead of later. Still, it was anything but pleasant to watch him spending most of his time with another girl at the cookout Saturday night.

Lisa had a good time, though, and Sondra was pleased to see several of the boys paying attention to both of her cousins. Obviously the two were dying to start dating, and Sondra hoped that Lisa would find a Jewish boyfriend in Kansas City who would keep her from going out with non-Jews in Lincoln.

The second week after school started Lisa announced to her parents that she was going to the Friday night dance, after the game, with Chris Wilson.

"No, you're not," her father countered. "No daughter of mine is going to start dating before she is sixteen."

"That's so unfair," Lisa raged. "You let Howie start dating when he was fifteen."

"And look where he is now!" Herbert roared.

"You can go to the dances with your girlfriends." Irene tried to pacify her daughter.

"Nobody goes to the dances with girlfriends. Everybody has a date."

"I never noticed your cousin, Sondra, going out on dates. She survived and so can you," Herbert growled.

"Oh, so now you're telling me I can't date at all, even after I'm sixteen."

"I'm telling you that I don't want to hear anything more on the subject until after you're sixteen. Is that understood?"

Herbert's accent was thicker than normal and that was a sign that he was really angry. Lisa knew better than to continue the conversation. If she changed the subject, Herbert's temper would end in a matter of minutes. If she kept on the same line, she would end up grounded. When Friday night came, she went to the dance with two other friends who had strict parents. Her father even picked them up afterwards and they came over to her house for a sleepover party.

Meanwhile, Sondra was settling into a routine of sorts. She had arranged her classes and work schedule so that she had Fridays and Saturdays off. Studying kept her busy, but not so busy that she did not continue to visit her grandmother daily. She also stopped by her aunt and uncle's house once a week and visited the store often. A couple of girls from school invited her to join in a lot of their weeknight plans. And every Friday Sondra would take off for Kansas City, taking Lisa with her as often as she could.

Debbie had been right when she had told Sondra that Shabbat in Kansas City would not be the same with so many of her friends away at college. Miriam, the rabbi's daughter, was still there and a few, who studied at the University of Missouri, came home often. Still, most of Sondra's time was spent at the Marcuses and Sondra got to know Mrs. Marcus well.

Contrary to what Debbie and the others had thought, Hannah Marcus did not just tolerate the youth group for her husband's sake. She enjoyed the laughter and the enthusiasm of the kids. Many of the outings her husband organized were her suggestions, taken from memories of what she had enjoyed doing when she was a teenager. Aaron Marcus had few pleasant memories to draw on. His teenage years had been spent in a small English village as part of the Kindertransport from Germany. Fortunately for him, he was reunited with his mother once the war was over. They had cousins in New York and the two of them had been able to immigrate to America. Aaron's mother, a talented seamstress, had supported the two of them while Aaron continued learning in yeshiva. He met Hannah, a native New Yorker, at a family party. Once they were married, he began teaching and became a successful teacher, the kind whom students remember for years afterwards.

After being married a year, the Marcuses had a baby boy and named him Nathan after Aaron's father. A bright boy, he delighted his parents with his quick aptitude for learning. They were eager for him to have a younger brother or sister, but it took ten years for Hannah to become pregnant again. When the baby, Leah, was born, she was severely retarded. Hannah and Aaron took her home from the hospital, determined to raise her at home. But the baby couldn't nurse, and she took hours to finish each bottle. She wasn't gaining weight. The pediatrician was not sympathetic. He had told them in the hospital that she should be placed in an institution. Aaron's mother agreed with the doctor. When Hannah came down with pneumonia, partly because of exhaustion, her family, except for her sister, also began to pressure them to put the baby in a special home. After a long talk with their Rabbi, Aaron and Hannah found a Jewish institution for Leah.

Hannah was depressed for a long time after placing the baby. She couldn't help but feel that had Aaron's mother and her own family been more supportive, they could have made it with Leah at home. She began to shy away from many of the family parties. Leah's institution was expensive and Nathan's tuition increased every year. A colleague told Aaron about job offers in out-of-town communities where the salary was incomparably higher than what was being offered in New York.

"Of course, there are a lot of disadvantages," the co-worker cautioned. "There's little *yiddishkeit* in most of these places. The teachers have to provide nearly all the authentic Judaism. You work hard for the money – doing everything from burials to reading from the Torah. And, of course, you're far away from your families."

It was the last point that appealed to Hannah. She and Aaron moved to Kansas City and when Nathan finished eighth grade they sent him back to New York, to Hannah's sister, for high school. Now he was learning in yeshiva in Israel. Leah had died before her fifth birthday. Over the years, Hannah had made peace with her family. There were times when she longed to move back east, to be in a community where more than three women covered their hair and did not go mixed swimming, but she felt that the work her husband was doing in Kansas City was too important to stop.

Chapter Twenty-Three

O f course, Sondra did not learn Hannah's entire life story in
one Shabbat. Bits and pieces came out as she taught Sondra
how to cut up a salad on Shabbat and still observe the laws of se-
lecting, or while she was explaining why the women did not *have*
to eat in the sukkah. Sondra listened to the explanations of the
laws of modesty and began to leave her pants in the closet more
and more. She saw that while Mr. Marcus worked well with the
youth, there were a number of women in the community who
came to his wife for advice. Sondra's respect for Hannah Marcus
continued to grow and, despite their age difference, she began to
think of her as a friend and a confidante.

It was Hannah who suggested that Sondra become the counselor for the junior-high kids in the youth group. That meant
having an activity for them every Shabbat afternoon as well as
helping Mr. Marcus with the motza'ei Shabbat entertainment.
Sondra entered into the work wholeheartedly and, like the youth
groupers, began to look forward impatiently to the Winter Convention that was going to be held in St. Louis.

"You've got to sign up to go," she urged Lisa on their way
home from Kansas City two weeks before the big event.

"I don't know," Lisa popped her gum. "I'm hardly going to
know anybody there."

"What about the kids from Kansas City?"

"I really don't know them that well."

"What about Rachel?"

"She's not going."

"She's not?"

Lisa shook her head. "She has cheerleaders' workshop that week."

Sondra took a deep breath, but did not let Lisa see how taken aback she was. "You'll have me there. I'll look out for you."

"Well, maybe I will go." Lisa agreed halfheartedly. "There won't be much happening at home that my folks will let me go to."

Lisa threw her gum in the car trash and laid her head back for a nap. Watching the turnpike carefully, Sondra stole glances at her sleeping cousin every so often. Lisa was no longer the eager ninth-grader who was interested in anything her cousin had to tell her about being Jewish. Now she was often bored by the subject. Sondra wondered whether it was Howie's death that had caused the change. But Lisa had been interested last year even after her brother had died. Maybe it was just part of adolescence. Sondra sighed and hoped that it would pass soon. She, at least, was looking forward to the Winter Convention.

She wasn't disappointed. The spirit and workshops were as great as she had remembered and it was fun being part of the staff. She met a counselor from St. Louis and they spent a lot of time together. He was a sophomore in the University of Illinois and was studying social work. He had also been to Israel after his high school graduation and was determined to go back for graduate school. They found a lot to talk about and at the end of the week Sondra promised to write to him.

Lisa had also found a pen pal. A good-looking junior wrote her five letters in the month of January alone. Lisa was flattered by his attention and told her friends she had a boyfriend in Des Moines who had his own sports car. She was a poor correspondent with him, though, and for his five letters she only wrote one. After several months he decided she wasn't really interested in him, and he met someone else at the Spring Convention.

Sondra kept her eyes on her cousin and was not too happy with what she saw. As she began wearing her skirts longer, Lisa's seemed to get shorter and shorter. Then there was the makeup. When Lisa started high school her mother let her wear a little blush and a light-colored lipstick. That was all Sondra ever wore, and only when she got dressed up. Now Lisa was wearing blush, lipstick, eye shadow, and mascara just to go to school. It was an unusually warm Thursday morning when Herbert voiced what Sondra had been thinking for weeks.

"You have such a beautiful face, Lisa. Why do you have to hide it with all that gook?"

"All the girls wear this much makeup," Lisa answered with dignity.

"Sondra doesn't and neither did Bernice when she was in high school."

"Well, I'm not Sondra and I'm not Bernice. And," Lisa added angrily, "I don't want to be."

"You look like a tramp," Herbert slammed his coffee mug down on the kitchen counter. "Go wash your face, now."

Silently, without any more arguments, Lisa did as she was told. She left the house sulkily without saying goodbye to her father. The beautiful weather did nothing to help her mood. Once at school, though, she went straight to the bathroom and remade her face with even more makeup than she had had on before.

She had been hanging out in the park with some friends for about an hour after school was over when Sondra, taking a shortcut, walked by. Sondra opened her mouth to greet her cousin, but Lisa's face showed that she was anything but pleased to see her. Quickly Lisa hid something behind her back, but not quickly enough. To Sondra's horror, she realized that she had caught Lisa smoking.

"What are you doing spying on me?" Lisa obviously had decided the best defense was a good offense.

"I'm on the way to visit your mother."

"Always Miss Goody-goody," Lisa snapped.

"Don't let me disturb you," Sondra said, unable to keep the hurt out of her voice. "We'll just pretend we didn't see each other."

"You mean you're not going to tell my parents?" Lisa raised her eyebrows.

Sondra just shrugged and walked away. She was in no mood to visit her aunt, though. And she was not sure what was the right thing to do. If it had been Howie who had discovered Lisa smoking, he would have cracked a few jokes, made Lisa promise never to smoke again, and Lisa probably would have kept her promise. Sondra knew that would not work for her. She wasn't cool enough. It was getting harder and harder to talk to Lisa. Sondra wished she could say she didn't care, but she did care a lot about what happened to her cousin. If she went to anyone in Lincoln for advice it would get back to Uncle Herbert or Aunt Irene and be like tattling. Suddenly Sondra remembered Hannah Marcus. It would be perfect to talk to her tomorrow.

Construction on the turnpike and then a simple errand at Aunt Lotte's that lasted half an hour more than it should have meant that Sondra got to the Marcuses only twenty minutes before candle-lighting.

"Oh, good, Sondra," Hannah sighed with relief when she opened the front door, "I was beginning to get worried about you."

"I'm sorry," Sondra apologized. "I should have called you from my aunt's, but I was afraid that would make me even later."

"It's okay," Hannah reassured her as she ushered her into the living room. "I want you to meet my friend, Rose Bennett."

Sondra smiled at the middle-aged woman sitting on the couch without showing her disappointment. There would be no heart-to-heart talk with Hannah about Lisa while Mr. Marcus went to shul.

Sondra knew Mrs. Bennett by sight from shul. She came most Saturday mornings, always wearing a tailored suit with a matching hat, shoes, and purse. Usually she sat in the middle section with her husband, a tall man with a surprisingly youthful face.

"You're Lotte Katzner's niece, aren't you?" Rose asked, totally oblivious to the frustration her presence had caused.

"Yes, I am," Sondra nodded. "Just let me put my things away and help Hannah with anything last minute."

"I don't need anything, but do you want to shower?"

"There's time?"

"For a fast one."

"Okay." Sondra quickened her pace. She threw her overnight bag into the guestroom, took the muktza items out of it, showered, and was dressed in time to watch Hannah light candles. Rose also lit a set of candles and Sondra wondered if she was going to be sharing the guestroom with her.

"You know, Sondra," Rose said as she relaxed on the couch. "I was a small town girl once, too."

"Really?"

"I grew up in Goodland."

"I didn't know that," Hannah said. "Were there other Jews there?"

Mrs. Bennett shook her head.

"Was it hard?" Sondra asked.

"You better believe it," Rose laughed.

"What kept you Jewish?" Hannah asked.

"Well," Rose thought for a bit, "I think it was two things. One was anti-Semitism. It was never overt, but I always felt it lurking under the surface. The other was that every year for Rosh Hashanah and Yom Kippur we would go to my aunt's in Denver and they would come to us every year for Seder."

"Did your parents let you date?" Sondra wanted to know.

Rose laughed. "My parents sent my sister and me to a Catholic girl's school. It wasn't like today. The nuns didn't let *anyone* date, although a lot of the girls sneaked out. Between fear of the nuns and fear of our parents my sister and I behaved ourselves."

"How did you and your sister meet your husbands?"

"Through relatives," Rose answered shortly.

"How are your courses going, Sondra?" Hannah changed the subject.

"Good, I'm doing a paper on raising children on kibbutz for my sociology class."

"I have a good book on that subject if you want to borrow it," Hannah offered.

"Sure!"

"Let me get it out of the study while there's still light."

Rose's smile had returned to her face. "What are you majoring in?"

"Education, with a minor in drama."

"Well, education is good and practical," Rose nodded. "You'll always be able to support yourself as a teacher."

"I guess so," Sondra agreed.

"Everyone should be able to be financially independent," Rose said. She smiled, but her eyes seemed sad.

Hannah returned with the book, and while Sondra looked through it, the two older women discussed the upcoming Sisterhood fundraiser. Mr. Marcus returned home and the Shabbat meal was pleasant, but rather rushed, as he had to return for the eight o'clock service. Rose continued to visit, even after they had finished cleaning up, and, although she wasn't sleeping over at the Marcuses, Sondra saw there was not going to be any time to talk to Hannah that evening.

She finally got her chance on Shabbat afternoon before the youth group activity, while Mr. Marcus was still sleeping. Hannah knew so much about Sondra's life that she did not have to explain too much more than what had happened at the park with Lisa.

"Tell me, Sondra," Hannah had listened patiently. 'What do you think your aunt and uncle are demanding from your cousin?"

Sondra twisted her ring. Just that week, she had overheard Aunt Irene tell her mother that she and Herbert often wondered how different Howie's life would have been if he had been as interested in Jewish things as Sondra was. Sondra could not tell Hannah that, though. Since the accident, she had not mentioned Howie to anyone outside the family.

"I think they want her to be more like me. More interested in Jewish identity and less in dating non-Jews."

"How does she feel about that?"

"I don't know. She's dying to date, but her parents told her she has to wait until she's sixteen. She's popular and she'll have no trouble getting dates once she is sixteen, but there aren't any Jewish guys to date. Her parents have let her know they won't be happy about her dating non-Jews."

"It sounds to me as if Lisa might be getting some pressure at home to be more like you and she's beginning to resent you."

"Could be," Sondra was skeptical. "But everyone in the family thinks my cousin, Bernice, is the perfect role model. Jewish, but not too Jewish. They're all afraid that I'm going to try to make all of them religious. As if I could! I don't think they want her to be like me. But she sure seems to resent me."

"So there is no point in your trying to talk to her about the smoking."

Sondra shook her head.

"And talking to your aunt or uncle would probably just finish the relationship."

"Probably."

"It's important to keep the lines of communication open. You never know when your cousin may turn to you again for guidance about being Jewish or anything. I wouldn't say anything about the smoking to anyone. From what you told me about Lisa's reaction she may very well feel guilty enough stop on her own."

"And if she doesn't and if she starts with drugs and…"

"Don't borrow trouble," Hannah hugged Sondra. "What you should do is pray a lot."

Sondra nodded. She remembered how she had prayed that Howie would not marry Patty. How would Hashem answer her prayers about Lisa?

165

Chapter Twenty-Four

On Thursday evening, Lisa sat in front of the television set, trying to concentrate on the programs, but her attention was really on the phone. She dreaded its ring, afraid that Sondra would be on the other end. There were several phone calls, but none of them were for her. The only one who came to the door was the paperboy. Lisa breathed a sigh of relief at ten-thirty when her father shut down the house. Once in bed, though, she had trouble falling asleep. The hurt look on Sondra's face made her feel guilty, and feeling guilty made her angry. She tossed and turned for over an hour and woke up Friday in a bad mood. When she left for school she couldn't help wondering if Sondra would stop by while she was gone. She was not eager to come home after school, and stayed at the drugstore as long as she could. As she finally opened the front door, she wondered if she was in for her father's rage and her mother's sorrowful looks. Nothing happened. It was obvious that Sondra had not tattled on her before she left for Kansas City. Lisa could enjoy her weekend.

She went to the movies on Friday night with her gang from the park. They sat in the back row, put their feet up on the empty seats in front of them, and made loud jokes while waiting for the movie to start. Once the cinema was dark, the cigarettes came out, but Lisa refused one. One of the girls laughed at her, but Lisa ignored her. There was no sense in spoiling her reprieve.

On Saturday, when they all went to the river, she again turned down a smoke.

"What's the matter?" Crystal Carson asked. "Are you afraid your weirdo cousin might appear?"

Lisa just shrugged. She had never liked Crystal and could never understand what the rest of her friends saw in the girl. Certainly not good looks, Lisa thought. Crystal was tall and skinny and had dyed blonde hair with brown roots showing. She had moved to town that year and Lisa doubted that her name really was Crystal, but there was no way she could disprove it. The one thing the girl had going for her was a permissive mother who let her daughter have friends over any time of day or night and never bothered to supervise them. There was going to be a party there that night.

Herbert dropped his daughter and her best friend, Cathy Miller, off in front of Crystal's tract house at nine o'clock that evening. He could hear the music blaring and was thankful he did not live next door.

"That sure is a lot of music for just a bunch of girls working on a science project," he said, looking suspiciously at his daughter.

"Our project is on noise," Lisa answered innocently. "Do you want to come in and check it out?"

Herbert shook his head impatiently. "Cathy, your mother's picking up before eleven, right?"

"Yes, Mr. Apfelbaum," Cathy smiled. She had one of those angelic-looking faces that made people naturally trust her. Herbert had known her since she was in fifth grade when she and Lisa became friends. She was as comfortable in the Apfelbaum's home as she was in her own.

The wine and beer were flowing freely when Lisa and Cathy walked in. And there were a lot of guys, many of them juniors and seniors. Cigarette smoke filled the air and there was another smell, very sweet, that Lisa did not recognize. It didn't matter, though. Right away one of the older boys asked her to dance. She was not bored for a moment. When she wasn't dancing, she was sitting and talking with some of the guys. She felt extremely grownup and when the elderly woman from next door came to complain about the music being too loud, she joined with the others in laughing at the neighbor.

At a quarter to eleven, Cathy tugged at her arm and said it was time to leave. Lisa rose reluctantly, hating her curfew.

She was looking forward to sleeping in Sunday morning, but at seven-thirty the phone next to her bed, on her private line, rang shrilly. It was Cathy.

"What do you want?" Lisa asked irritably.

"Listen, this is important." Cathy sounded wide-awake. "Crystal's neighbor called the police because of the noise last night and they came about midnight and there were kids smoking marijuana and they were arrested and it's on the front page with a picture of Crystal's house and the name and the address, and as soon as your parents see the paper they're going to know all about it and want to interrogate you just like my parents, so we have to get our stories straight."

"Wow," Lisa took a deep breath and sat up. "Okay, what did you tell your parents?"

"I told them that we were there for the science project like we said, but after ten a few guys stopped by, but we didn't know anything about marijuana and it must have started after we left."

"Didn't it?"

"No, I smelled it as soon as we walked in."

"Really?" Lisa whispered. "How did it smell?"

"Really sweet."

"Oh." Lisa swallowed. "Well, your story is fine. They know your mother picked us up before eleven. You say the police did not come 'til an hour later. We should be fine."

"As long as you stick to the story and they don't go asking too many questions."

"Well, I'll tell Karen and you tell Peggy. I don't think they'd ask any of the others."

169

"Okay," Cathy agreed. "Good luck."

Lisa replaced the receiver and made her phone call. She tried to fall back asleep, but that was impossible. How come her parents were not banging her door down? Usually her father was up early and out at the ranch first thing in the morning. Should she go out there and face them? No, that wouldn't be acting natural. If they hadn't heard the phone ring, they would be expecting her to sleep 'til noon. She read, dozed, worried, and checked her watch every fifteen minutes as long as she could. Finally, at eleven, hunger pangs drove her from her room.

"Good morning, dear," her mother looked up from her book. "Did you sleep well?"

Lisa nodded.

She was halfway done with her Rice Krispies when she heard her father come in. There was a serious conversation in the family room and then, Herbert and her mother walked into the kitchen together. The morning paper was in her father's hand.

"We want to talk to you." Herbert was not angry, yet. "What happened here last night?" He pointed to the picture of Crystal's house.

Quickly, looking straight at her parents, Lisa repeated the story Cathy had told her.

Her father and mother nodded. It was clear they wanted to believe her.

"I don't want you to have anything to do with this girl again, do you understand?" Herbert spoke calmly.

"Yes, Daddy. I never liked her anyway," Lisa spoke truthfully. "Just the others wanted to be nice to her because she was new in town."

"Find someone else to be nice to."

Lisa couldn't believe how easily her story had been accepted. She walked over to Cathy's that afternoon and the two went for a long walk. Both marveled at the good luck that they had to have such trusting parents.

"We're going to have to come up with a science project," Lisa pointed out. "My parents are going to want to go to the science fair."

"Okay," Cathy nodded. "We can do that. Let's go to the library after school tomorrow."

"Should we ask Peggy and Karen to help?"

"But just them," Cathy nodded. "None of the others. Listen, Lisa," Cathy wrung her hands. "I feel like a real jerk lying to my parents. You might think I'm a real retard, but I'm going to be careful what I do from now on. I hate sneaking around."

Lisa nodded her head in agreement. "Me, too. I was angry with my folks for not letting me date, but if we had been there last night we could have been arrested. Wow, would that have been a mess. If my father stops trusting me I might as well hang it up. He'll make my life miserable and ground me till I'm twenty-one."

"So we'll stick up for each other if the others laugh at us?"

"Sure."

Lisa was extremely pleasant that evening at dinner and began loading the dishwasher without being asked.

"Did you finish the science project?" Irene asked as she cleaned the table.

Lisa shook her head. "It wasn't a good idea to work Saturday night. We barely got anything done. We're going to go to the library tomorrow after school."

The phone rang before her mother could reply. Lisa tensed up. Was the call about the party?

"It's Sondra," Irene handed her daughter the receiver.

"Hello," Lisa's voice was full of apprehension.

"Hi," Sondra sounded friendly. "I just wanted to tell you that Rachel gave me a Carole King record for you. I was too tired to bring it by tonight, though."

"That's okay," Lisa was contrite. "It was nice of you to let me know. You do a lot of nice things for me."

"You do a lot for me, too," Sondra answered. "I'll see you tomorrow."

"Okay." As Lisa hung up the phone, she tried to think of anything nice that she had done for Sondra lately.

Chapter Twenty-Five

*A*lready a month before Passover, Sondra had received three invitations for the Seders: one from the rabbi's family, one from Debbie, and, of course, one from the Marcuses. She hadn't seen Debbie since winter break and was anxious to be with her, but she was the most comfortable with the Marcus family. And, after all the Shabbats she had spent in their home, she felt a responsibility to be there to help Hannah. Of course, Rose Bennett would there to help out.

Since Sondra had first met her, Rose had been eating almost every Friday night at the Marcuses. She was not interested in becoming religious. She always parked her car down the block. After helping Hannah clean up from the meal and visiting with her until Mr. Marcus came home from the second service, she drove home. In the mornings, she would drive to the shul and afterwards meet some friends for a game of Mah Jongg.

Sondra no longer davened in the sanctuary upstairs, but rather in the chapel with the divider separating the men and women in the basement. She had not realized that Mrs. Bennett's young-looking husband no longer sat next to her in the mixed section. In fact, he was no longer in her life at all. He had asked for a divorce six months earlier and was planning to marry his secretary.

Poor Mrs. Bennett had married straight from her parent's

home in Goodland. The only time she had ever earned a salary was when she had been a teenager and worked in her father's clothing store. Since she had no children, she was getting the bare minimum in alimony. Hannah had found her a job working as a receptionist at the old-age home, but she was forced to live frugally. Rose came to the Marcuses every week to socialize and boost her self-confidence, which had suffered badly in the past year. Sondra had grown to like her more and more each week. She loved hearing Mrs. Bennett's stories about growing up in Goodland. Rose had liked growing up in the small town and it was too bad, Sondra thought, that she couldn't move to Lincoln and take over Mrs. Ward's job. Sondra had made the suggestion to Hannah one Shabbat afternoon, but her idea had not been well received.

"She needs as much emotional support as she can get now. Moving to a new town would be too stressful. Who would look out for her, besides you? Here she has me, and her Mah Jongg group, and her neighbors, and friends in the sisterhood. What she really needs is a new husband, and that's why Aaron invited his lawyer for first night Seder. He lost his wife two years ago."

Intrigued by the matchmaking scheme, Sondra had made up her mind to go to the Marcuses for the Seders, but when she came home Sunday there was a letter from Debbie waiting for her.

"As of now, we're not having any guests for our Seders. Since this is my brother's last year in Israel he isn't coming home either. We were invited out for one night, but I like being home. So do my parents and if you come we'll have an excuse not to go out. Please come," Debbie had ended her letter.

Full of indecision, Sondra refolded the letter and stuffed it back into the sky-blue envelope. Impulsively she turned to her mother for advice.

"What do you mean, you don't know where to go for Seder?" Helga asked. "This year we're going to Aunt Irene's first night and everyone is coming here second night."

"I thought I was going to be in Kansas City," Sondra answered in a small voice. She glanced at her mother and saw that she was not angry, only hurt.

"Families are supposed to be together at the Seder," she said softly. She abandoned her lecture notes and retreated into her room.

Sondra sat down at the kitchen table and tried to sort out her thoughts. Her parents had been great about her being in Kansas City for the High Holy Days and they hadn't said a thing about Sukkot or Simhat Torah. Of course, they barely celebrated Sukkot and Simhat Torah. She had just taken it for granted that she would spend most of Passover away.

She wondered how it would work if she did stay with the family for Passover. Not driving wouldn't be a problem. It would be a long walk from Lisa's, but she could manage it. Her mother and Aunt Irene changed their dishes for the week, but Sondra knew that they did not do anything near the amount of cleaning that Hannah and Mrs. Greenbaum did. Would their food really be kosher for Passover? At worst, she could survive on fruit, salad, and *matza*. She knew Uncle Herbert's Seder was going to be boring. Like every year, they would read through the Hagaddah as quickly as possible in order to get to the meal. Still, like her mother said, there was something special about families being together for the Seder. Sondra swallowed hard. She would stay home for Passover and make her parents happy.

It wasn't as bad as she had thought it was going to be. Aunt Irene had a self-cleaning oven and Sondra was able to eat the gefilte fish, the turkey, the stuffing, the salads, and the fruit. True, the Seder was not spiritually uplifting, but there were a lot of interesting family stories told as they sat around the table. When it was over, Sondra slept in Lisa's guest bed. No one wanted her walking by herself so late at night and no one wanted to walk with her. The next day, Lisa accompanied her on the walk home and Sondra appreciated her company.

Lisa was making a big effort to get along. She sat with Sondra as she made a yom tov meal that lasted much longer than Julius's lunch break. She listened to stories that Sondra had heard at the Marcuses' table. She even took a Haggadah and read the grace after meals in English. Later, she helped Helga and Sondra get ready for the second Seder, but once that was over she drove home with her parents. She had a test the next day and was not interested in taking off any more time, even to be nice to Sondra.

The second day of Passover passed slowly for Sondra. She could not believe that she had once spent Shabbat after Shabbat at home. She missed going to shul and she missed being around the table with others who wanted to sing and talk about the holiday. Her parents did sit with her for lunch, but Sondra couldn't really call it a seudah, a special meal. Her father had to hurry back to the store and her mother had an afternoon lecture, so Sondra finished by herself. She had just begun to clear the table when there was knock on the kitchen door.

"I decided to take my lunch break here," Oscar said as he made himself comfortable at the dining room table.

"Do you want some gefilte fish?" Sondra tried to act as if Oscar stopping by for a meal was the most natural thing in the world. It was obvious, though, that she was surprised by his visit.

"Sounds good," he grinned. "You're trying to figure out what I'm doing here, and the truth is that I want to talk to you."

"Okay," Sondra handed him a full plate and sat down across from her cousin.

Oscar busied himself with his food, taking his time, as always, to begin speaking.

"It's not good you being here," he finally spoke, shaking his head. "You feel guilty that you're alive and Howie's dead. I know, I felt the same way for years after the war. Because of that I never lived my life fully."

"I live my life fully!"

"No, you don't," Oscar shook his head adamantly. Now that he had made up his mind to talk there was no stopping him. "You're young and should be having good times with young people. What do you do? You go visit your grandmother every day. You stop by the store and visit me every week. You check in on your aunt and uncle. You look out for your little cousin. Even when you go to Kansas City you're with old people. Once in a while you go to a play or the movies with a couple of girls. And you read books. That's not a full life." He shook her finger at her. "You need to get out of here. I want to see you going to the University of Colorado next year. You've served your time here."

Oscar's face softened and he smiled at Sondra who was biting her lip and trying to blink back tears. "It was good what you did this year. You helped all of us a lot. But enough is enough. Go live your life."

"What about you?" Sondra asked defiantly. "When are you going to live your life?"

Oscar waved his hand impatiently. "It's too late for me. I'm almost fifty years old."

"That's not too late," Sondra shook her head adamantly. Suddenly she was inspired. "Oscar, I know a woman who would make a great wife for you." Before he could object she began describing Rose Bennett.

"She sounds very nice," Oscar conceded, "but what would she want with someone like me?"

"Oscar, you're a good, honest, caring person."

"I don't know," Oscar laughed sheepishly.

"Oscar," Sondra laid her hands flat on the table and took a breath. "If you try taking Mrs. Bennett out three times, I promise to go away for college next year."

"Well," Oscar hesitated. "You don't give me any choice. I guess I'll go visit Lotte and Manny Sunday. You can come with and introduce me to this woman. I sure hope you know what you're doing."

177

Chapter Twenty-Six

"*E*xcited?" Debbie asked as she fastened her seat belt.

"Scared." Sondra pushed her carry-on bag under the seat in front of her.

"Scared?' Debbie repeated. "You've flown before."

"Yeah, I'm not scared of flying. I'm just terrified about going so far from home," Sondra said sheepishly.

It had been just four hours earlier that she had boarded the bus in Lincoln. Both her father and mother had been there to see her off with big smiles. From the window, though, Sondra saw both of them holding handkerchiefs to their eyes and she had to blink back tears herself. There had been some real tears the night before at Oscar's, when she said good-bye to her Oma and the others. Rose had invited all the family for a going-away dinner.

Oscar had kept his end of the bargain. After meeting half a dozen times he had asked Rose to marry him and, to everyone's delight, she agreed. The scowling, angry man that Sondra remembered as a little girl had totally disappeared. Although he was still a quiet man, Oscar's laughter was often heard. And whenever any of the family heard his laugh, they forgot their irritations with Sondra's religious ways and blessed her for being such a successful matchmaker. With such a warm welcome from all of Oscar's relatives, Rose's self-esteem blossomed. She took over the Apple

Children's Department with so much confidence that even Uncle Simon could not find fault with her.

Following Oscar's talk with her, Sondra had gone to Kansas City for the last days of Passover. Mr. Marcus and Hannah had been thrilled with the bargain she had made. In no time they had convinced her to apply to Stern College, and no one had been surprised when her acceptance came. Sondra had been ecstatic then, but now she knew the only thing keeping her on the plane to New York was that Debbie sat in the aisle seat and would demand an explanation if Sondra got up.

"It will be fine," Debbie reassured her.

"I know," Sondra laughed somewhat nervously. "Did you get a lot of teasing about being from Kansas last year?"

"Some," Debbie admitted. "I played along with it and told them my father always walks around with a six-shooter. One girl believed me. Can you imagine my father as a cowboy?"

Sondra had to laugh at the thought of Cantor Greenbaum with his scraggly beard and thick glasses dressed up like Clint Eastwood. "Maybe that's what he should be next Purim."

"Right," Debbie made a face. "As if my father ever dresses up for Purim."

Sondra laughed again and suddenly felt relaxed. "I'm sure glad you're with me. I hope I don't become a pain in the neck at Stern, but I'll probably be asking you a million questions every day."

"Don't be silly," Debbie shook her head. "I'm thrilled you're coming. You're my best friend."

Sondra smiled. Debbie had never been stingy with her feelings, but it sure felt good to have their friendship reaffirmed. She was glad they were going to be roommates.

The two other girls in their room were also out-of-towners. Suzie Singer from Memphis had been in Debbie's room the year before, and Libby Marcus from Philadelphia was a transfer student like Sondra. For the first week Sondra felt as if she were at a Shabbat convention. As papers became due and examinations scheduled, the atmosphere became more serious, but still, almost everyone in the dorm cared deeply about yiddishkeit. Sondra may have felt different because she was from Kansas or a *baalat teshuva*, someone from a non-observant home, but there were dozens of girls keeping kosher and observing Shabbat just like she did. The youth group in Kansas City could not compare to the Stern College dormitory.

The four girls in Sondra's room all forged a strong bond. They shared a number of lovely Shabbatot together, as well as books, boxes of cookies, and evenings out. Many a time Sondra would find herself convulsed with laughter from their good times, and suddenly she would wonder if she had recovered from Howie's death. It certainly did not hurt as much as it once had. She thought about it less and she never talked about it. Debbie was the only one who knew she had lost her cousin, and Debbie had learned that it was a taboo subject for Sondra.

She did have one problem with New York, though. No matter what direction she looked, she always saw more and more buildings. The city made her feel claustrophobic. An occasional walk in Central Park helped a bit, but it wasn't safe to go there alone. It could not compare to a solitary ramble in the pasture.

Her favorite classes were on Jewish subjects and after several months, and a talk with the placement counselor, she decided to change her major to Judaic studies and make education her minor. That same evening, Suzie brought up the subject of spending their junior year in Israel.

"My oldest sister did it three years ago and my other sister last year," she announced. "It's a given that I'm going, but it sure would be nice if you all would come, too."

Intrigued Sondra put down her textbook and stared at Suzie. Debbie stopped writing and bit her lower lip thoughtfully. Libby just laughed.

"Do you have any idea how much work it was to get my parents to let me go this far away from home? Fat chance I'd have to make it to Israel."

"About forty percent of the junior class goes," Suzie said.

"I spoke to my parents about it in the summer," Debbie said. "They're open to the idea, but I'm not sure if I want to go. Where did your sisters learn?"

"One was in Machon Gold…"

"Where's that? Sondra interrupted.

"Jerusalem."

"Did they learn in Hebrew or English?"

"There are different programs. My other sister learned at the Michlalah."

"What's that?" Sondra asked.

"It's a teachers' college in Jerusalem."

"If I go to Israel," Debbie picked up her pencil, "that's probably where I'll go. But enough talk. I have to finish this paper tonight."

Libby returned to her math equations and Suzie to her chemistry formulas. Sondra reopened her textbook, but found she could not concentrate on anything. She decided that she needed to talk to the counselor again as soon as possible.

Sondra was able to make an appointment the following day and left the office starry-eyed. Since she had so many secular credits from Lincoln State, there would be no problem with her devoting a year to Jewish studies. The counselor had given her the brochures about Machon Gold and the Michlalah. While Sondra looked them over, the older woman had drummed her fingers on her desk and looked Sondra over carefully.

"I have an idea that might be better for you," she announced.

Sondra looked up questioningly

"A friend of mine is starting a *midrasha* of Jewish studies, for young women who have some background but who were not raised religious. We, here at Stern, will accept the credits and

182

I think it will serve your needs more than the other two places, which assume all of their students are FFBs, *frum* from birth."

Sondra smiled at the abbreviation for observant from birth. She knew that she and Libby were referred to as BTs. She listened carefully as the counselor described the program and decided it was perfect for her. Now she had to convince her parents. The counselor could not help her with that, though.

There really was no one at Stern who could give Sondra advice. Debbie was the only one who had ever met her parents. Even though their mothers had both survived the camps, that was about the only similarity the two women had. For a day Sondra toyed with the idea of calling Cousin Richard. She had dutifully called him when she first arrived in New York. He had been cordial and graciously invited her to meet for lunch at a kosher restaurant, but his busy calendar did not fit in with Sondra's class schedule. Besides, Sondra reasoned, he had never lived in Lincoln when her parents had. He could probably give her as much advice as Debbie could.

Wistfully, she remembered all the times she had turned to Howie when she was troubled. She couldn't turn to Howie now. That thought made her shed a few tears, but she resolutely wiped them away and thought of Bernice. She was only a few hours away. Surely Libby would know the train schedule. Sondra could go for the day and have a heart-to-heart talk with Bernice.

Libby did better than give Sondra the train schedule.

"My parents have been after me to come for a weekend. Shabbos is not all that great there so I've been pushing it off, but if you come with me we can make Shabbos together. My house is close to the shul. We'll be invited someplace for lunch. And on Sunday morning I can drive you over to your cousin."

Chapter Twenty-Seven

The two cousins had not seen each other in well over a year. Last summer, Bernice had cancelled her annual visit and missed Uncle Simon's birthday party. Instead, she had stayed home and nursed her two toddlers through chicken pox. When Bernice called her uncle to wish him well, it was Sondra who had answered the phone. Thrilled to be able to talk to her cousin, Sondra took the chance to tell Bernice all about Rose and Oscar's upcoming marriage. Bernice gave the right responses, but Sondra had sensed a drop of resentment in her cousin's voice. It made sense, Sondra had thought as she called Uncle Simon to the telephone. Of course Bernice felt like she was missing out, being so far away in Philadelphia.

"Do you ever get homesick for Kansas?" Sondra asked as they were cleaning up from lunch. Robert had taken the girls to the playground.

"More than you can imagine," Bernice answered.

Sondra looked closely at her cousin. She had put on a lot of weight with both of her pregnancies, and even though the youngest was already two, it did not look like Bernice had lost any of it. As she thought of the macaroni and cheese that they had just eaten, it did not seem to Sondra as if Bernice was trying to lose any, either. And she had cut her long, beautiful hair into a short style that was easy to take care of, but did nothing to flatter her.

Sondra sensed that Bernice was not happy, and she nervously searched for something harmless to say.

"Sometimes in New York I feel like I'm going to suffocate if I don't get any fresh air," Sondra said.

"I got over that." Bernice began loading the dishwasher. "What I really miss is being my own person."

Sondra gave her a puzzled look.

"Everything I do here is scrutinized by Robert, his parents, *and* his grandparents. You're thrilled that I keep a kosher house and you can eat here, but that was never my decision. It wasn't even Robert's decision. We were ordered."

Sondra felt her face flush as she tried to think of something tactful to say.

"You see these dishes?" Bernice held up a flowered, china plate. "They're not my taste. I wanted earth-tone pottery, but this is what Robert's grandmother picked out for us and this is what I have to use."

"Oh."

"I want to go back to teaching next year, and I found a good day-care center for the girls, but Robert's mother is having a fit. 'No grandchild of mine should be in day care,'" Bernice mimicked her mother-in-law.

"What does Robert say?"

"He tells me to do what I want, but he never defends me to his parents." Tears began rolling down Bernice's cheeks.

"Oh, Bernice," Sondra swallowed. "That's too bad. Maybe we should sit down."

"I'm sorry." Bernice grabbed a tissue from the counter as she sank into a kitchen chair.

Sondra sat down across from her cousin. As Bernice pulled herself together Sondra surveyed the kitchen. It was tastefully decorated and full of conveniences, but Sondra was afraid to give any compliments. Perhaps the entire kitchen was from the grandmother.

"I'm sorry," Bernice repeated as she blew her nose and wiped her face. "You didn't come all the way from New York to hear me complain about married life."

"Is it all so terrible?" Sondra asked nervously.

"Not all," Bernice answered honestly. "But it's not happily ever after like a fairy tale, either."

"Don't you think your mother would be telling you what to do all the time if you were living in Lincoln?"

"Maybe," Bernice shrugged. "But I wouldn't feel obligated to always listen to her. Robert's family can't seem to make a separation between the time that Robert is their employee and the time when he has his private life."

"Kind of like Uncle Simon." The moment the words were out of Sondra's mouth she regretted them, but Bernice just gave her a knowing look.

"Yes, like Uncle Simon, but my mother knows how to stand up to him when it matters. Did you know he didn't want to give her vacation time when Carrie was born? Mom told him she was coming to help me and if he didn't like it he could fire her."

"Really?"

Bernice laughed. "As if he would fire her. She's too devoted a worker. He'll have a fit when she finally decides to retire. But enough about my family problems. Tell me about yourself."

Sondra described the dorm and how nice it was to live with a bunch of girls who cared about Shabbat and keeping kosher.

"It's great not having to explain myself all the time. And I love the Jewish studies, and that's the real reason why I wanted to come see you."

"Yes." Bernice waited.

"A lot of the girls do their junior year in Israel. I found this great program for me there, but I don't know how I'll approach my folks about it. Any suggestions?"

"That's something to think about," Bernice nodded her head. She rose and brought a bag of chips and some diet soda to the table.

"Do you think your parents can swing it financially?"

Sondra nodded. "I think so. We still haven't touched the money from Germany."

"Are you willing to use that money and go without their approval?"

"No," Sondra shook her head immediately. "I don't mind using the money, but I won't go against their wishes."

"You should tell them that," Bernice said. "When you first bring the subject up. That you won't go without their blessing."

"Okay. And then what do I say?"

Bernice munched on a handful of chips and thought over Sondra's question.

"You're far past the stage where you could say you need to go to Israel for Jewish identity. They probably wish you didn't have so much Jewish identity."

Sondra nodded ruefully.

"But Israel really is not that much farther than New York. Okay," Bernice answered Sondra's skeptical look. "It's across the ocean, but New York isn't a day's drive away like Oklahoma or Colorado Universities. They let you come this far. The thing that would stop your parents, I think, is the danger in Israel."

"So I'll have to answer their fears for my safety."

Bernice nodded. "But you can't give any guarantees. Look, Howie was killed right outside Lincoln."

"Yeah," Sondra bit her lip.

"I think that's your answer," Bernice took a long swallow of her Tab. "If God wants you dead it can happen anywhere. Even in the shower you can slip on a bar of soap and hit your head and die. Tell your parents that you won't go without their approval. Tell them that you can die anywhere. And tell them that for your personal growth and development, you need to go to this program. If you don't, it will be something you'll regret for the rest of your life. More than anything, they want to see you happy."

"So does your mother," Sondra said.

"I am, most of the time," Bernice answered.

Chapter Twenty-Eight

Sondra made the decision to push off her conversation with her parents until Hanukkah break, when she could do it in person. Then she spent the first few days home, nervously waiting for the perfect opportunity. Her father had already begun working long holiday hours at the store and her mother was absorbed in getting grades ready. Sondra kept herself busy visiting her grandmother and all the other relatives. On Thursday evening, some of her friends from Lincoln State, anxious to escape studying for finals, invited her to join them and go out for drinks. Touched that they still thought about her, Sondra accepted the invitation.

They went to Archie's, a new pub that catered to the college crowd. Lacquered spool tables, sawdust on the floor, dim lights, and a folk singer in the corner made for a laid-back atmosphere. The conversation around their table was laid back also. Even though Sondra did not understand all the references to current affairs on the campus, she felt relaxed, at least until a group of five high-school students entered.

"Look at them," one of the girls nodded her head. "It's so obvious they're underage. How did they get in?"

"Fake IDs are a cinch to get."

Sondra's back was to the entrance, but she turned around and found herself looking straight at Lisa.

Her cousin had matured a lot since the previous year. She

was still wearing more makeup than Sondra ever would, but it was applied tastefully. And although her sweater was low-cut, it was not too tight. Sondra was certain that Uncle Herbert had seen his daughter leave the house and had approved of the way she looked. Sondra was also certain that he did not know where she was headed.

"Hi, Sondra," Lisa said pleasantly. There was none of the antagonism that had been in her voice when Sondra had caught her smoking a year earlier. "I'm surprised to see you here."

"I'm sure you are," she answered. "I'm surprised to see you, too."

"Don't worry," Lisa smiled. "None of us are going to get drunk. We came for the music."

"Sure," one of the guys said and everyone laughed, including Lisa.

"No, really. Mike's brother is the singer and we want to give him moral support."

"That's really considerate," someone said.

"It is," Sondra agreed. "Does Uncle Herbert know you're here?'

"No," Lisa answered lightly. "But he knows the only interesting hangouts in Lincoln are the ones for the university crowd and they all serve beer."

"Then I won't mention that I saw you," Sondra spoke good-naturedly. Not a hint of the concern she felt for her cousin was seen on her face or heard in her voice.

"Thanks. I'll see you Sunday at the Hanukkah party."

Sondra silently watched her cousin join her friends. For the first time she felt a twinge of doubt about her plans for next year. Perhaps she should stay closer to home and keep an eye on Lisa.

"Don't worry about her," one of the girls gave her hand a reassuring pat. "I did the same thing when I was in high school."

Even with Howie gone, Aunt Irene still made her Hanukkah party. With his *yahrzeit* coming up that week though, the accident was the main topic of conversation, and everyone left feeling thought-ful.

"It's always so sad when a young person dies," Helga shook her head as she fastened her seat belt. "Howie had so many dreams and plans."

"He was happy in high school." Julius meant to be comforting. "He was on the team and the student council and was popular."

"Irene told me how he always wanted to go to Germany and see where his parents grew up. He also wanted to see Israel. And he so wanted to be a veterinarian. He did not get to do any of it." Helga sighed.

Sondra realized that this was probably the best opportunity she would ever have.

"Mom, Daddy," Sondra spoke up from the back seat. "I have a dream that is really important to me, but I'm not going to do it without your approval and blessing."

Calmly and slowly, Sondra explained the program and why it was important to her. "I know you're worried about my safety there, and if you let me go I'll be sensible and not take risks, but if God wants me dead, it can happen anywhere."

Helga exhaled audibly. She hadn't realized she had been holding her breath ever since her daughter mentioned Israel. She looked at her husband, who was navigating the turn past the barn.

"We thought you would have gotten Israel out of your system from the summer before last," he said as he parked the car.

"I guess I didn't."

"Well, give your mother and me some time to chew this over and talk about it."

The next day Sondra regretted that she had ever mentioned the subject of studying in Israel. Helga went through her routines do-ing all she normally did, but she did her work without a smile and almost no conversation. By Tuesday, Sondra could no longer stand it and borrowed the car to go to the store. Julius only nodded at her when she walked in. He had a customer who was buying his teenage son his first suit. Even though she knew it would take a long time, Sondra did not wander off to visit with Oscar or Rose, or even to check out what was new in the dress department. She leaned against the sock counter and waited patiently.

Finally, after giving his customer change, Julius turned to his daughter.

"Hi, honey," he gave her a kiss. "What brings you here?"

"I'm worried about Mom," Sondra said simply. "I guess I shouldn't have said anything about wanting to go to Israel."

Julius sighed and took a handkerchief out to wipe his brow. Sondra looked closely at her father and was surprised to see so many gray hairs on his head. For the first time she realized that her parents would one day be old.

"It's hard for your mother," Julius agreed. "You know, let's go sit down and talk this over. Bill," Julius called to his assistant, "I'm taking a coffee break."

They sat in the first booth at Molly's. As Julius stirred the sugar in his cup he began speaking.

"You know your mother, well, both of us, want what's best for you. Lincoln's not best for you. We always knew that. We always thought you'd end up close by in Kansas City or Wichita or even Tulsa. But I guess, now that you're so Orthodox, you don't want to live in any of those places, right?"

"Not really," Sondra spoke softly. "I bet you wish I'd never met Mr. Marcus."

"Well," Julius laughed, "if I had my druthers I would have had you go to the University of Colorado and meet someone traditional like Robert and settle somewhere in the Midwest. We had always hoped you'd follow Bernice's path, but I do prefer what you're doing to what Brenda did."

"Okay," Sondra said. She did not mention the problems she had seen in Bernice and Robert's household.

"So what do we do now?" Julius shook his head. "We had

hoped you'd be happy in New York, but we were afraid that you'd find it too big to be comfortable."

Sondra nodded.

"You gave us good reasons for wanting to go learn in Israel. We're going to let you go. We already decided that Sunday night. But it's hard for Mom. It's so far away and she's going to miss you so much, and worry about you, but she said first that you should go. Now she has to get used to the idea. Be patient with her."

"She said I should go?" Sondra could not keep the excitement out of her voice.

"Yes."

"And you think it's okay?' Sondra stammered. "You don't think it's going to break her heart or anything?"

"No," Julius smiled. "She'll be okay and so will I. We're putting two conditions on you, though."

"What?"

"You'll write every week and you're coming back at the end of the year."

"Okay," Sondra agreed seriously.

From Molly's she went to visit her Oma, and when she got home her mother was setting the table for dinner. Helga greeted her daughter with a smile and Sondra felt a sense of relief. She wondered if her father had told her mother about their conversation at Molly's, but she knew she would never ask. She was just thankful that her mother was not going to make her feel guilty for following her dream.

Once back at Stern, Sondra took the first weekend possible to go to Philadelphia with Libby. Again, she spent Sunday with Bernice and thanked her for her advice. This time Bernice served salads for lunch.

She confided to Sondra that she was on a diet and going to Weight Watchers. Also, she had signed a contract for teaching and, at her insistence, Robert had told his parents and grandparents that it was their joint decision that the girls would be in day care next year. Sondra made several more visits to Philadelphia during the school year. Each time she went, Bernice was a little bit slimmer.

Bernice and her family were able to come to Lincoln for their summer vacation. However, there was no party for Uncle Simon. He had suffered a stroke the month before and was lying in the hospital, hooked up to all sorts of tubes.

"It's only a matter of time," Aunt Irene told the relatives who had gathered at Berta's.

Hearing that made Sondra feel badly. Even though he had been really angry with her for refusing to work on Shabbat, once his anger was spent he had been as good to her as ever. Always a fighter, Uncle Simon was still alive two months later. Sondra wondered if he would die while she was in Israel. That would be sad, but it would not keep her from going. She spent the summer working in the library again, and then it was time to begin packing. The following week she would be on the plane for Israel. She was so excited she could barely contain herself.

Chapter Twenty-Nine

"Sondra," Debbie squealed from inside the crowded pizza shop. "I'm over here!"

Sondra's searching eyes relaxed and she broke out in a smile and her dimple deepened.

"Is Suzie here yet?" Sondra asked after they had hugged each other.

"Not yet, but you know how she's always late. Let's go ahead and stand in line so that by the time she gets here we can order."

They had just reached the head of the line when Suzie came bounding in, her long, black hair flying behind her.

"Debbie, Sondra, sorry I'm late." She caught her breath and hugged both of them at once. "You look great."

"So do you," Debbie answered and they broke into laughter. It had been less than a week since they had last seen each other, but what a week it had been.

"It's too crowded in here to talk," Suzie declared once they had their pizza in their hands. "There's a park a few blocks down. You want to go there?"

Debbie and Sondra nodded and the three navigated their way out of the shop.

It was motza'ei Shabbat and downtown Jerusalem was packed. There were soldiers on leave, university students, young teenagers, married couples, and a large number of overseas students. It had been Suzie's idea for them to get together their first Saturday night. "My sister told me that the phone situation in the seminaries is impossible. Let's just make up to meet half an hour after havdalah."

"So, tell us all about Shaarei Bina," she demanded as soon as they were settled in the park.

"It's great," Sondra beamed. "Rebbetzin Feingold is so down-to-earth. I feel like I can ask her any question I want without feeling embarrassed. The lectures are good. There are sixteen girls from all over, South Africa, England, and there's even a girl from Holland. How's it going for you guys?"

Both girls nodded enthusiastically.

"Machon Gold is just what I expected from everything my sister told me," Suzy said

"I like the Michlalah, but my roommate is driving me crazy," Debbie admitted. "She's born and bred in Long Island. Her English is fine and her Hebrew stinks, but she insists on talking to me in Hebrew. And after I've finished learning all day in Hebrew, that's the last thing I want to do. Today I told her to go practice her Hebrew with the Israeli students and she was insulted. She wouldn't sit with me at lunch," Debbie shrugged.

"Did she sit with the Israelis?" Suzie asked.

"Don't know," Debbie shrugged again.

"One of my roommates is driving me crazy, too," Sondra offered.

"How?"

"She wants me to explain everything I do that isn't exactly what she does."

"Like what?"

"Like yesterday, I opened a bag of pretzels before candle-lighting so I wouldn't have to worry about making a container or tearing the words when I wanted to eat them this afternoon. So, she had to know why I did it since you're allowed to tear for food and by the time I finished explaining to her all the hot water was gone and I had a cold shower."

"Yuck," Debbie laughed. "How long has she been a *baalat teshuva*?"

"About six months. Why?"

Suzie and Debbie exchanged glances.

"That's the way most *baalei teshuva* act the first year," Suzie explained.

"Did I act like that?" Sondra demanded of Debbie.

"Kind of," Debbie made a face. "But you never drove it into the ground."

"Gosh," Sondra faltered. "I guess I better be more patient. Tell us about you," she demanded of Suzie.

"Everything's what I expected, except that they already started talking about matchmaking at an informal lecture this afternoon."

"Really?"

"We're not getting any younger," Suzie answered with a laugh.

They could have talked for hours, but each of them had a curfew. So they parted before midnight with the promise to meet again the following motza'ei Shabbat. Sondra returned to the dorm determined to be more patient with Stephanie.

The twenty-four-year old nurse was from Chicago and had become interested in yiddishkeit while working with a religious family whose son had leukemia. She was a sensitive woman who still got tears in her eyes when she spoke of the boy's death, but she did not seem to have a sense of humor. Sondra had thought Stephanie would find her laughter frivolous, but for some reason she sought out Sondra's company. In fact, when Rebbetzin Feingold paired the girls up to go out to families for *yom tov* meals, Stephanie asked to go with Sondra. For Yom Kippur they were placed with a young British family in the Bayit Vegan neighborhood of Jerusalem.

"Go early," the rebbetzin had instructed them. "The buses stop running early."

On the way home from Kol Nidrei, the city was unbeliev-ably quiet and Sondra was overcome with a sense of peace. She left for shul early the next morning, *mahzor* – the holiday prayer book – in hand, with every intention of spending the whole day in prayer. It was during *minha*, the afternoon prayer, that she first heard the sirens and she prayed that whoever was on their way to the hospital would be okay. But the sirens kept going over and over again. She noticed that the women near the front seemed agitated and at the break the word spread that someone had come inside the shul to call up the soldiers. Israel had been attacked!

For those still in shul, the service, already eloquent, became much more powerful. Sondra found herself sobbing by the time the shofar was blown at the end of the day. "*Leshana haba'ah bi'Yerushalayim habenuya*," next year in Jerusalem rebuilt. What would be the next year? Or even tomorrow?

Back at her host's home, the father made havdalah and turned on the radio as his wife put food on the table. The news did not sound good. Sondra and Stephanie ate a little, helped clean up, and made their way back to the seminary. The atmosphere on the bus was somber. Rebbetzin Feingold was waiting for them at the dormitory when they arrived.

"Girls," she instructed, "You must call your parents first thing in the morning, as soon as Yom Kippur is out there. Come to my apartment when you get up."

"Can I come at five?" Sondra was hesitant to ask.

"I'll be up," The rebbetzin nodded. "Is that when you want to call?"

Sondra nodded. "My parents go to sleep early."

"That's fine. Also girls, your Sukkot vacation really begins tomorrow. The country is going to need all sorts of volunteers. Think about what you want to do to help out."

Sondra's conversation with her mother had not been easy.

"Don't you think you should come home?" Helga pleaded.

"Mom," Sondra tried to reassure her over the phone. "Jerusalem is safe. No one is leaving. And I can help out here. I'm going to be delivering mail. Most of the postal workers were called up to the army."

As a guest in the country, Sondra did not feel the war the way the Israelis did. There were occasional air raids where they had to run for the nearest bomb shelter, but to her knowledge nothing ever hit Jerusalem. After Sukkot, classes resumed normally and she did her postal route during break time. She had no friends in the army, and she and Debbie and Suzie continued to meet for pizza every motza'ei Shabbat.

It wasn't until the family who lived next to the dorm lost their son that Sondra began to feel the war personally. She had seen him once on Shabbat, a tall, handsome boy with fringes hanging out of his uniform. His mother, a seventh-generation Jerusalemite, brought cake over to the girls every erev Shabbat. Sondra made a shiva call with a few of the girls, but she was too overcome with emotion to say anything besides the phrase of comfort that is said as one leaves a shiva house.

That night she dreamed of Howie's funeral. She woke up to Stephanie gently shaking her.

"Shush, you're having a bad dream. Here," she handed Sondra a tissue, "dry your face. Do you want a drink?"

"I guess so," Sondra faltered. "I'm sorry I woke you. What about the others?"

"They don't have my sixth nursing sense. They haven't stirred."

She tiptoed into the kitchen and came back with a glass of juice.

"I guess the shiva call upset you." Stephanie spoke soothingly, as she would speak to a patient.

"I guess so," Sondra agreed, and tried to fall back asleep.

Chapter Thirty

*F*inally, a cease-fire was reached, although Sondra felt none of the euphoria she had felt at the end of the Six-Day War. Many of the soldiers were coming back from the front and life for the Israelis was returning to a semblance of normalcy. Sondra had given up her postal route and had stopped calling her parents every Sunday. Now she wrote to them weekly and in turn received newsy, green aerograms from Helga three or four times a week.

On Wednesday, her mother had written that Jane was engaged to a divinity student. Sondra could imagine them moving to some foreign country to convert the "heathens." It would be a dream come true for Jane. She just hoped they would not move to Israel. There were plenty of stories about missionaries giving out money and food to poor Jewish immigrants in order to convert them. For a few minutes, Sondra considered writing Jane a letter of congratulations, but dismissed the idea. They really did not have anything to say to each other.

She tore open the next aerogram from her mother right before candle-lighting on Friday. It was a full one, with every space taken up with Helga's tiny handwriting. Sondra stuffed it in her pocket to read later when she had time. After cleaning up from dinner, most of the girls went for a walk, but Sondra stayed behind and curled up with the letter and the latest Victoria Holt mystery that Suzie had lent her. She never got to the mystery that evening. Helga's letter contained the news that Bernice and Robert had separated.

"For the meantime, Bernice is in the house and Robert has moved in with his parents. There is talk about Bernice coming back to Lincoln when school is out and moving in with Berta and getting a teaching job here. Talk about history repeating itself! Except there won't be one male in the house. Bernice at least had her grandfather for a father figure. Her girls won't have anybody if they go through with this. I sincerely hope that they work things out. Poor Berta is so upset."

The letter continued with inconsequential news and concluded, as usual, with the fact that there was no change with Uncle Simon. No mention of how Bernice was feeling. Was she heartbroken, relieved, glad? Who had initiated the separation? How were the girls reacting? Dozens of questions went through Sondra's mind. If she had still been at Stern, she would have planned to visit Bernice on Sunday. If she were in Lincoln, she would have gotten permission to call her cousin on motza'ei Shabbat. But, she was in Israel and a visit was impossible and a phone call was too complicated and expensive. Sondra remembered the wedding and how happy Bernice had been. She also remembered how Bernice had told her that married life was not happily ever after like a fairy tale.

For some people it was, though. Sondra felt certain that her parents were as happy together as they had been when they first married. And even though Aunt Irene and Uncle Herbert had lost a son, they were still happy with each other, or so it seemed. The Marcuses were happy, Sondra was certain of that, and they had lost a child, too. She did not know the Feingolds well enough to judge their happiness, but Rebbetzin Feingold had already given them a number of talks about the sanctity of marriage. It wasn't just at Suzie's seminary that the girls were encouraged to go out on arranged dates. Sondra had not been able to decide if she thought the idea was exciting or frightening. Now she found it only frightening.

Tired, Stephanie came back from the walk before the others, who had stopped off to visit the rebbetzin. She was surprised to see her normally smiling roommate looking depressed.

"What's the matter?"

"Oh," Sondra gave a nervous laugh, "I was reading my letter from home and my cousin just separated from her husband. I feel so bad for her."

"I'm sorry," Stephanie said sincerely.

"Everyone here is telling us to get married and then we hear so many people are getting divorced. I don't know what to think."

"I think," Stephanie spoke adamantly, "that there is a big difference between religious marriages and non-religious marriages."

"Maybe," Sondra conceded. "But my parents are not religious and they have a good marriage."

"They were from the past generation," Stephanie shook her head. "It's a world of difference. Their generation knew what commitment was."

"I guess so," Sondra agreed halfheartedly. What about Rose's first marriage, though? she thought. "Well, it's Shabbos," she said resolutely. "I'm not going to think about this any more 'til tomorrow night."

The following night she was sitting inside a coffee shop with Debbie and Suzie. The days of eating pizza in the park were long gone. Now they sipped hot tea while wearing sweaters and long underwear. And it was just the beginning of winter.

"What's happening with you guys next Shabbos?" Debbie asked.

At Shaarei Bina the girls were expected to be in the dorm and eat together once a month. Also, once a month, they were expected to sleep in the dorm and to eat with the families in the neighborhood where Rebbetzin Feingold placed them. Twice a month they were allowed to go where they wanted as long as the rebbetzin approved, but if they wanted to stay in the dorm she would make meal arrangements for them. Already Sondra had been to Aunt Irene's relatives on the kibbutz and, to her delight, she had discovered that the relatives she had been with for Tisha b'Av lived a block away from the seminary. Sondra had eaten a number of meals with them and was invited to their son's wedding next month.

"I have no plans. Why?" Sondra asked.

"I'm finally going to the family that sort of adopted my brother when he was here and I'd like some company. Any takers?"

Suzie shook her head. "I promised my roommate that I'd go with her to her cousin in Bnei Brak."

"I'll come with you," Sondra agreed. "Where are we going?"

"They don't live that far from my dorm, so if you sleep by me we can walk back and forth. I think they have a really tiny apartment. My brother used to sleep in the living room."

"Okay," Sondra agreed. "As long as I get permission."

The Rosens' apartment was tiny. An American couple with married children who had moved to Israel before the Six-Day War, they welcomed overseas students into their home week after week. There were ten people crowded around the dining room table that had been opened up and extended into the living room. Before the meal was over, just as Mrs. Rosen and her daughter-in-law were bringing dessert to the table, there was a knock on the door.

"Hi, Gabe. Hi, Danny," Moishie, the Rosens' eight-year-old grandson, opened the door. "You guys always know the right time to come."

"Chocolate cake?" Mrs. Rosen asked.

"Sure!"

"Debbie, Sondra, please meet Gabe Segal and Danny Klein. Danny, Gabe, meet Debbie Greenbaum and Sondra Apfelbaum."

"Hello," Debbie smiled modestly.

Sondra, uncharacteristically, asked a question. "Klein. Are you, I mean, is your father by any chance from Germany?"

Danny shook his head and smiled mischievously. "My father's from Topeka."

"Topeka!" Both girls shrieked.

"You've heard of it?" Danny was clearly surprised.

"I'm from Kansas City," Debbie exclaimed, "and Sondra's from Lincoln."

"You're more of a hick than I am," Danny grinned at Sondra.

Mrs. Rosen quickly explained Kansas to her South African daughter-in-law.

"Do you come to Kansas City often?" Debbie asked, eager to play Jewish Geography.

"Not really," Danny answered sheepishly. "You see, we left Topeka when I was starting high school. My mother's arthritis got worse and my father thought Phoenix would be better for her, so we moved. Gabe here is from L.A."

Mr. Rosen cleared his throat, ready to give a talk on the weekly Torah portion. After they recited the grace after meals, the four young Americans got a chance to talk together. The boys stopped by again for *seudah shlishit*, the third meal, and stayed to help clean up. On Wednesday afternoon Rebbetzin Feingold called Sondra into her office with a very serious face.

"I got a phone call from Leah Rosen who, as I told you, is an old friend of mine. She tells me that a boy who eats by them often, Danny Klein, stopped by Friday night and he is interested in going out with you."

"Really?" Sondra blushed and smiled in spite of herself, her left dimple deepening. She had liked Danny's friendly brown eyes, his sense of humor, and the way he had of constantly rearranging his suede yarmulke on his curly brown hair.

"Really," Rebbetzin Feingold could not help but return Sondra's smile. "However," she spoke fondly, "this is not America. Going out is not to have a good time. It is for the purpose of marriage. Are you ready for that?"

"I don't know," Sondra faltered.

"Think about it. I told Leah I would not get back to her for at least a week. Take your time. I'll be here to talk to. This is an important decision."

Chapter Thirty-One

"Wow!" Suzie's voice was louder than Sondra would have liked. "You're going to be the first of us to be married!"

"Shush," Sondra flushed. "I haven't even decided if I'm going to go out with him yet…"

"But you will," Debbie interjected. "It's so fantastic. Two religious Kansans meeting in Jerusalem. It's got to be made in heaven."

"Be serious," Sondra implored.

Neither Debbie nor Suzie meant to be so unsympathetic, but both were giddy from midterms. They had looked forward to their weekly meeting as a chance to unwind and not to have a staid discussion. Sondra got no advice from them.

The next evening, though, Stephanie, having noticed how preoccupied her roommate was, approached Sondra.

"Is your cousin still on your mind?"

"Which cousin?" Sondra was puzzled.

"The one who's separated."

"No, well," Sondra faltered, "I guess she is, in a way."

Slowly, Sondra explained her conversation with the rebbetzin. Stephanie was a good listener. Her eyes sparkled as Sondra described Danny, but Sondra did not see that reaction. She was too busy fiddling with her ring.

"I think that's great," Stephanie exclaimed once Sondra finished talking.

"But I don't know if I'm ready for marriage," Sondra cried.

Stephanie smiled. "What are your goals in life?"

"To have a Jewish home, of course. Until last year, I thought maybe I would be a drama teacher, but now, maybe, I'd like to teach Jewish studies. And I don't know where I want to live. My parents made me promise that I'd come home at the end of the year, but maybe I'll want to come back to Israel to live, but I don't know if I could do that to them and the rest of the family. There are so many question marks in my life."

"But your first goal is to have a Jewish home, right?" Stephanie pressed.

Sondra nodded.

"It's a hard thing to do alone. If I were you, I'd go out with this guy and try it. You're not sixteen years old. Lots of people get married when they're twenty."

Sondra thought over Stephanie's advice. "Have you spoken to the rebbetzin yet about a shidduch for yourself?"

"Oh, yes," Stephanie tone was rueful. "It's not going to be easy to find a match for me."

"Why?"

"I'm a twenty-four year old *baalat teshuva* divorcee. Who…"

"You were married!?!"

Stephanie just nodded.

"Why don't you cover your hair?"

"I wasn't married to a Jew."

"Oh," Sondra nodded, trying to reconcile her view of her roommate with what she had just learned. "What happened?"

"He was not mature enough to handle the commitment that marriage needs. I was married at twenty-one, divorced at twenty-two, and became religious at twenty-three."

"How can you – of all people – recommend that I start going out?"

Stephanie surprised Sondra by laughing. "Sondra, you're

prime for marriage. You've been religious for three years. Your main goal in life is not some career but rather building a Jewish home. You're open to where the future will take you. You have a strong commitment to family. This boy, Danny, may be your intended and he may not. The only way you're going to know is by going out with him. If it doesn't work, nothing is lost, except for maybe some studying time, but you can always make that up."

"Well," Sondra faltered. "I'll think about it."

That was about all Sondra thought about for the following forty-eight hours. Tuesday afternoon she came home from classes to find a jackpot of mail on her bed: three aerograms, one from her mother, another from Rose and Oscar, and, surprisingly, one from Lisa. It was Lisa's that she opened first, and she was treated to gossip from Lincoln High.

"Do you remember my friend, Cathy? She and her boyfriend were just crowned homecoming queen and king. I was one of her attendants and if they get married I'll be the maid of honor, but I hope they don't get married. They'll probably just get divorced. I don't know why anyone bothers to get married anymore.

I guess your mom wrote you about Bernice. It will be kind of neat to have some young relatives in town for a change. I was the only person under forty at Mom's Hanukkah party.

Everyone is receiving answers about their college applications. Rachel is going to the University of Missouri. My boyfriend is going to University of Arizona and I've been accepted at Arizona State University. It's in Tempe, right outside Phoenix. The brochures look great. There are palm trees all over the campus. Do you have palm trees there? I'm really excited. Tempe is about an hour and a half drive from Tucson where the U of A is. I'll be able see Tim a lot.

Dad's calling me to go out to the ranch with him. I'll

mail this on the way. It would be really cool if you write me back.

Lots of love, Lisa"

Sondra didn't know whether to laugh, cry, or be angry about the contents of her cousin's letter. Boy, were they worlds apart in their outlook on life. But it made her sad that Lisa's view of marriage was that it wasn't worth having. She wished she could explain to Lisa the beauty of so many of the marriages she had seen among young couples in the religious community. But Sondra realized that while she was unmarried there was nothing she could say to Lisa. It was at that moment she decided to tell Rebbetzin Feingold that she was ready to go out.

Chapter Thirty-Two

They met in the lobby of the King David Hotel, where Sondra drank the most expensive orange juice she had ever had. Somehow, it was not as easy to talk in the lavish surroundings as it had been in the Rosen's crowded apartment. Searching for a topic of conversation, Sondra remembered Lisa's letter.

"My cousin wrote me that she got accepted at Arizona State University. Is that near you?"

"It's about a forty-five minute drive," Danny fiddled with his yarmulke "I've been there for some concerts and the science fairs. It's a really pretty campus."

"Is there much of a Jewish presence?"

"A lot of the Jewish kids in Phoenix and Scottsdale go to ASU. And there's a bunch of Jewish New Yorkers who come for the sunshine. Is a Jewish presence important to your cousin?"

"I don't know," Sondra laughed regretfully. "I want it to be important to her. When she began high school she really cared about being Jewish. But then she got fascinated with all the social life there and the two do not really go together if you're the only Jew in the whole school."

"How did you manage?" Danny was interested.

"My cousin, Lisa's brother, was in my class and so we kind of supported each other."

"Does he care about Jewish things?"

"I don't know." Sondra studied her ring as she turned it round and round her finger. "He left home in our last year of high school. I miss him." Sondra swallowed her last drop of orange juice and tried desperately to think of a new topic of conversation.

"Maybe we should go for a walk," Danny suggested.

Sondra nodded and pulled on her woolen coat and gloves.

Automatically, without consulting each other their feet headed in the direction of the Old City.

"What made you decide to become religious?" Danny asked as they strolled towards Jaffa Road.

"Growing up in Lincoln I always felt different. I mean, I was different. There I was, in the middle of America, in the Bible Belt, almost everyone had been in Kansas since World War I, at least, and I had two immigrant parents, my first language was German, and I wasn't supposed to eat bacon or pork."

"Does your family keep kosher?"

Sondra nodded. "What about yours?"

"Are you kidding? My family is so assimilated that they had shrimp cocktail at my sister's wedding."

Sondra's jaw dropped open.

Danny laughed at her surprise. "In Topeka, being Jewish for us meant that we went to the Temple on Rosh Hashanah and Yom Kippur night and had a Seder of sorts at my grandmother's. It was just luck that my sister married a Jew. Do you want to go to the Kotel?"

"That would be nice," Sondra agreed. "So what made you decide to become religious?"

"When we moved to Phoenix my parents joined the Jewish Community Center. That was the extent of our Jewish commitment. But I met some Jewish kids at high school. You see, in Topeka there were five other Jewish kids my age in town, but only two of them went to my grammar school, and even though I could eat whatever I wanted and my parents were Americans, I still felt different. So in Phoenix I looked for Jewish friends. And it's amazing, even though most of them couldn't have cared less about being religious, they all cared about being Jewish and looked out for each other."

"So?" Sondra prodded him to continue as they entered Jaffa Gate.

"So they invited me to go with them to Hebrew High, which was an educational program at the Community Center. You could learn Hebrew and there were other classes taught by different rabbis in the community. One of the Reform rabbis taught Jewish history and there was a class about the Holocaust. I signed up for Hebrew and a class about *Mishna*. The guy who taught it was a teacher at the day school and he invited all the students to come to him for Shabbos. Two guys and I went. I think we need to turn down here."

Sondra followed Danny down a dark, quiet alley, a surprising contrast to the loud, bustling Arab market that she had always seen in the daylight.

"How was that Shabbos?"

"I loved it! Especially the cholent!"

"The cholent?" Sondra laughed.

"Yes, the cholent," Danny laughed with her. "My mom was on a vegetarian kick then and I was thrilled to have some meat. The other two guys never came back, but I did and then others from the shul – there were only about ten families then – also invited me for Shabbos, and by my last year in high school I was by someone every week for Shabbos."

"That's kind of like me." Sondra explained about all her Shabbats in Kansas City, until they came to the Kotel.

"I didn't daven yet this evening," Danny said. "Do you mind if I do so now?"

"That's fine."

"We'll meet there," he pointed to the back of the plaza, "in twenty minutes, okay?"

"Great," Sondra glanced at her watch and entered the women's section. Her heart was racing with excitement. Since leaving the King David Hotel there had not been one awkward silence.

She could not believe how easy it was to talk to Danny. She was anxious for the twenty minutes to pass so they could talk some more.

They met again three nights later, this time at a modest coffee shop on Ben-Yehuda, in the middle of downtown. There were none of the awkward silences there had been at the King David. Danny was eager to tell Sondra all about himself and she was eager to listen.

He explained how his grandfather had made it west from Romania via France, England, New York, St. Louis, and Topeka, picking up a wife and the medical profession along the way, but at each stop losing more and more of his *yiddishkeit*. It was in Topeka that he became one of the founding doctors of the hospital and that was where he decided to stay. Danny's father was born in St. Louis, but all of his memories were of Topeka. From the time he could walk he would follow his father as much as he could, determined to be just like him when he grew up. Although his parents named him David, everyone called him Doc. And Doc expected his son to feel exactly about the medical profession as he did.

"For my dad," Danny straightened his eyeglasses, "being a doctor is like a religion. He gets as excited about suturing a patient as I do about understanding a page of gemara."

"Do you want to be a doctor?" Sondra asked.

"I really like the idea of helping Hashem to cure a sick person. I like that a lot. But I don't know if I have the drive to finish med school, internship, and residency *and* keep up with my learning."

"There are a lot of frum doctors," Sondra said gently

"I know," Danny agreed. "But most of them grew up religious. I have a lot of learning to make up. My parents agreed that I could take a year off and dedicate it solely to learning. But only a year. They're hoping that after this year I'll be content to stop learning gemara and just concentrate on med school."

"And?"

"I hope I never stop learning, but maybe after a full year of only learning, I will be satisfied with fewer hours. I don't know." Danny shook his head.

Chapter Thirty-Three

"So," Debbie asked. "How's it going with Danny?"

"Nice," Sondra blushed. It was Saturday night and they were in their favorite coffee shop downtown. "Uh, I don't think I'll make it next motza'ei Shabbat."

"Why not?' Suzie was indignant.

"Danny wants to take me to a concert."

"Ohh, I guess you'd rather be with him than us," Suzie teased. "This must be getting serious."

"Suzie, stop it," Debbie took pity on Sondra's blushing face. "Do you think it is serious?" she asked earnestly.

"I like being with him," Sondra answered. "I look forward to his phone calls."

"He gets through at the dorm?"

"Not usually," Sondra admitted. "I go to the pay phone on the corner every evening at 8:15. He calls me after davening."

"You speak to each other every day?"

"Almost." Sondra could feel herself blushing again.

"What do you find to talk about?"

"Oh," Sondra hesitated, "all sorts of things." She felt that she had told Danny almost everything about her life that was worth telling. Almost, but not all. Somehow, she could not bring herself to talk about Howie's death, or how he had changed in high school or about their plan to find the Sefer Torah. Danny had the vague impression that Howie had dropped out and was living in some commune in California. Sondra said nothing to change that idea.

"Don't you think, that I should meet him?" Suzie asked. "I can't give you any advice if I don't know him."

Sondra laughed at her friend. "You know, my aunt once told me that she was dating someone before she married my uncle. He wanted to marry her and she wasn't sure, so she asked her brother, and he told her if you need to ask, then he's not for you."

"Are you telling us that you're sure about Danny?" Debbie looked at her friend seriously.

"Uh," Sondra faltered, "maybe I am. I guess, I mean, I'll see what happens."

The next day Sondra took a deep breath and wrote about Danny to her parents. Two weeks later Rebbetzin Feingold called her into the office. She had a phone call from home.

"How are you, dear?" Helga's speech sounded more accented than Sondra remembered.

"I'm fine," Sondra answered, her voice quivering. "Is it Uncle Simon?"

"No, no," Julius answered quickly. "Everything is fine here. We just want to hear some more about this young man."

"Oh," Sondra relaxed her grip on the phone. "I think I wrote you everything."

"Is it serious?" Helga asked.

"I think so," Sondra smiled into the phone. The rebbetzin noticed that Sondra's left dimple had deepened.

"Do you mind if we ask Aunt Lotte to check up about him." Julius asked. "She has some friends in Topeka."

"That's fine."

"I wish we could meet him," Helga said wistfully.

"Would you like me to send you a picture?"

"I guess that would be better than nothing."

"You'll like him when you meet him," Sondra reassured her parents.

They took another two minutes to give Sondra the news from home and then hung up. Not only was it an expensive call, there was a lot of static on the line.

Two days later Sondra got called out of class again. Again, her parents were on the phone and again, they assured her that all was well in Lincoln. However, they informed her, Helga and Irene would be flying to Israel in two weeks. They had decided that Helga, at least, should meet this Danny Klein before their daughter made any lifetime commitment.

Sondra hung up the phone feeling sheepish, indeed. Would meeting her mother make Danny feel she was trying to push things along? Was she? Maybe she should not have told her parents anything yet. She was glad her mother was not coming alone, but sure wished her father was coming, too. The biggest question was what she would tell Danny.

They met that evening and, with eyes downcast, Sondra mentioned that her mother and aunt were planning to come in for a visit.

"Do they want to meet me?" Danny asked.

"Well, yes," Sondra blushed.

"Great," Danny grinned. "I want to meet them. My parents are coming for a visit, too. They really want to meet you."

Sondra burst into laughter. "When are they coming?"

"They're waiting for the Pesah break."

"My mother and Aunt Irene are coming two weeks earlier."

"Um," Danny took a sip of his coffee and sat silently for a few moments. "Sondra, I think it would be a good idea if our folks came in at the same time. Then, if everything works out okay, we can become engaged. What do you think?"

Sondra did not say anything. She just smiled and that was the only answer Danny needed.

Although it took a bit of organizing, it was finally agreed that the parents would make their reservations for after Purim. Although Danny and Sondra were not officially engaged, they saw or spoke to each other every day. Two days before Purim he told her that he would be going to Haifa the next afternoon, even though it was a fast day.

"A friend of mine needs to get the paperwork done for his lift and his Hebrew is practically nonexistent. I told him I'd help him out, but I should be back before the fast ends. Will you be up to going to the phone?"

"Sure," Sondra answered. "I usually don't have any trouble fasting."

The next evening she was at the phone promptly at eight-fifteen. Fifteen minutes had passed and there had been no ring. An older man came by and asked her to move. She begrudgingly stepped aside while he made his call. Thankfully, he had a short conversation. After another five minutes of waiting, Sondra settled herself down on the curb. Jerusalem nights were still cold and she was decidedly uncomfortable. At a quarter to nine, Sondra tried dialing the pay phone at the yeshiva. It was busy and it stayed busy for twenty minutes. Finally, Sondra got through, but the person who answered the phone could not find Danny Klein and he did not strike her as a reliable messenger. At a quarter past nine, she finally gave up and made her way back to the dorm. Chilled through, she was thankful there was hot water. She showered, curled up in her bed with a cup of tea and a good book, and tried not to worry.

It was after ten-thirty when there was a knock on the apartment door. Stephanie, who was up studying and still dressed, went to the door.

"Who is it?" she called out in Hebrew.

"Danny Klein. Is Sondra awake?"

"Just a minute. I'll check."

Before Stephanie could turn around, Sondra was already flying out of her room tying her robe around her as she came.

Smoothing back her hair, she opened the door wide. Danny stood there dirty, disheveled, and undeniably apologetic.

"I'm sorry about tonight. I just got back."

"Is everything okay?"

Danny swallowed and nodded his head. "But I want to talk to you. Can you come out for a walk?"

Instinctively Sondra glanced at her watch. They had a ten-thirty curfew on weeknights.

"Go ahead," Stephanie urged. "I'll cover for you." It was obvious that Danny had something important on his mind.

"Okay," Sondra nodded at Danny. "Give me two minutes to get dressed."

She threw on a denim skirt, turtleneck, tights, and boots and grabbed her coat and a clip for her hair. They left the apartment without a word and headed toward a nearby playground.

"What happened?" Sondra demanded once they were settled on the park bench.

"Everything was fine until the way back. Right before Netanya there was an explosion on the road." He held up a hand at Sondra's gasp. "I think it was a terrorist bomb, but I don't know for sure. Anyway, it caused a huge accident. We just missed being in it. But we got out to help. There were six people injured. One was already dead. And one of the injured, a little boy about ten, was losing blood so fast. I made a tourniquet for him and when the ambulances got there and they got to him, they told me I'd saved his life."

"That's wonderful, Danny," Sondra said softly.

Danny nodded. "Sondra, I think Hashem means for me to be a doctor. Are you willing to put up with all that means?"

"What does it mean?"

"It means I won't be able to learn all day. It means that for the next few years, I'll be so busy finishing med school and learning, that probably the only time we'll see each other is on Shabbos. Are you willing to put up with that?"

"You won't be the first frum person to become a doctor,"

Sondra reminded him. "And I won't be the first person to marry someone going through med school. If we want it badly enough we can make it work."

Danny looked at her earnestly. "I want it."

"So do I."

They smiled with relief at each other.

"They told me at UCLA I could come back when I finished my year here in Israel. How do you feel about living in Los Angeles?"

"What's the frum community like?"

"It's not like New York," Danny admitted. "But there are a lot of religious families. A lot of young couples. There are several large shuls and a number of little minyans. There's some learning, although I would like more. It's not Jerusalem, that's for sure. The bakery's great, though, and there are a couple of restaurants and several schools. It's a big place, and. I don't want you to feel like you're suffocating like when you were in New York."

"It won't be forever, will it?"

"I hope not," Danny shook his head. "What I'd really like to do is come back here."

"Me too," Sondra agreed. "We can handle the smog for a few years if we're in it together."

Chapter Thirty-Four

"So, when do you want to have the wedding?"

Danny and Sondra smiled serenely at each other. The two were sitting at a round table in the coffee shop of the Moriah Hotel, where Danny's parents were staying. His parents were sitting next to him and Helga was next to Sondra. Irene sat between Helga and Shirley, Danny's mother. Sondra noticed that her aunt was every bit as elegant as her mother-in-law-to-be was. The engagement party had been held the night before at the yeshiva, but it had been just a formality as far as Danny and Sondra were concerned. Ever since the night of the accident, they had been certain that they would marry. Fortunately, their plans were mutually acceptable to their families and everyone was getting along.

"We thought the first week after Shavuos," Danny said.

"And then," Sondra continued, "we'd fly back to the States the first week in August, right after Tisha b'Av, and get settled in L.A. before school starts."

There was a prolonged silence that Irene finally broke.

"Are you thinking about getting married here?" she asked noncommittally.

Sondra and Danny nodded.

"I guess you don't want your father to be at your wedding?" Helga said sarcastically.

"You mean Daddy won't be able to get someone to milk the cows for a week?" Sondra flushed.

"And I guess you don't want your sister, Daniel," Shirley spoke before Helga could answer. "You know they can't afford a trip to Israel."

"What we thought," Danny spoke calmly, "is this. Weddings here are so inexpensive, compared with weddings in America, that the money saved could be used for airline tickets. Think about it."

"I don't want my son getting married in a cheap wedding," Shirley spoke decisively.

Helga shook her head. "Even if your father did find someone to take care of the dairy, you know good and well that he and Oscar and Rose and Berta would never be able to take all that time off together. I know you want Oscar to be at your wedding, don't you?"

Sondra nodded and exchanged looks with Danny. Irene was impressed with how much the two seemed to be able to communicate just with looks.

Danny cleared his throat. "Well, I did want to finish out the whole year, but I guess we can come back at the end of June and have the wedding before July 7th."

"What happens on the 7th?" Doc asked.

"It starts the three weeks before Tisha b'Av, a period when there are no weddings," Danny explained.

"I see," Doc nodded. It was clear to Sondra that Danny's father was a listener.

"I don't know, Danny," Sondra said. "I hate to see you miss out on your last month of learning here. We can stay 'til right after Tisha b'Av, have the wedding the middle of August, go straight to L.A., and you can start classes."

"I don't want to wait another two months," Danny objected.

"How about," Doc chose his words carefully, "coming back with us now, our present, getting married right after Passover, when you're still on break, returning here, and finishing up your year, and then getting settled in L.A.?"

Again Sondra and Danny exchanged looks.

"I'll talk to the Rosh Yeshiva."

"Who's that?" Irene asked, confused.

"The rabbi who's the head of the yeshiva."

"When can you have an answer from your rabbi?" Helga asked.

"I hope tonight."

"Do you think," Shirley turned to Helga diplomatically, "that you can make a wedding in such a short time?"

"I don't know," Helga laughed. "I've never made a wedding before."

Sondra envisioned the few wedding pictures from her parent's wedding and spoke quickly.

"We really want a simple wedding, Mom."

Danny nodded in agreement.

"Well," Irene interjected, "let's start planning right now." She pulled a pad of paper and pen from her purse. "First of all, we should talk about the place."

There was another prolonged silence.

"How about the Temple in Topeka," Shirley finally suggested. "It's not far from Lincoln, and even though it's not convenient for our friends in Phoenix, it would be perfect for my mother-in-law and our old friends."

"Mother," Danny spoke patiently. "We need a place that is kosher."

"Danny, none of our friends and relatives care about that. We can order frozen kosher meals for you and Sondra."

"No," Danny answered firmly. "We are not going to come back from Israel to get married at a non-kosher wedding."

"I think, perhaps," Helga interjected, "that the shul in Kansas City, where Sondra spent so much time, would be the perfect place."

Sondra gave her mother a grateful smile. She and Danny exchanged looks and nodded together.

The Rosh Yeshiva gave his blessing for a wedding right after Passover and plans were set in full motion. Gabe and Debbie would be going home for Passover and staying for the wedding. The rest of their friends would come to the post-wedding parties in Israel. Although it was not going to be the yeshiva wedding they had envisioned, Sondra felt confident that Hannah and Mr. Marcus would do their best to make it as joyful as possible. The rest of the week was spent in finalizing plans.

When Sondra and Danny tried to make reservations, though, they found that all of the direct flights were full and they would have to make a stop somewhere in Europe. That suited Sondra fine. She had an idea of her own that she shared with Danny on their way back to the travel agent.

"Instead of going through Switzerland," said Sondra, nervously playing with her new engagement ring, "I'd like to fly by way of Frankfort and take a few hours to visit my parent's village."

"You want to go to Germany?" Danny bit his lip.

"Just for a few hours," Sondra repeated.

"I don't know." Danny fixed his yarmulke. "The thought of going into Germany gives me the creeps. And I certainly don't want to support their economy."

"I know," Sondra sighed. "We'd bring our own food. But we would have to pay the train fare."

"The train fare?"

"There's a train from the airport to all the villages. It takes about an hour."

"How did you find all this out?"

"I called back yesterday."

"This really means a lot to you?"

Sondra nodded. "I would never have thought about doing it by myself, but if you're with me, well," she laughed nervously, "I think I could handle anything the trip brings me."

"How can I say no to that?" Danny shook his head. "I guess we have to stop in Europe anyway. What's a couple of hours?"

The travel agent was even less impressed with Sondra's idea than Danny had been, but she made their reservations. It was obvious Helga was having an emotional struggle about her daughter's plan to go to Germany, but she did not say anything.

That evening Sondra said goodbye to her mother and Irene, as their flight was leaving in the middle of the night. She and Danny would be leaving first thing in the morning.

Chapter Thirty-Five

The flight was uneventful. After a full week of being almost constantly with their families and talking practically nonstop about wedding plans, Danny and Sondra were happy to have some time alone. It was good to be able to talk about anything but wedding plans. When Sondra closed her eyes to for a much-needed nap, Danny pulled out his gemara and enjoyed learning.

Sondra awoke with the pilot's announcement to fasten seat belts. As they landed, Danny clasped his hands tightly and kept his apprehensions to himself. Sondra's heart was beating wildly as she hoisted her flight bag over her shoulder. They had checked their luggage on through to New York. Danny unzipped his carry-on and put the gemara on top of his tefillin bag. The doors to the plane opened and they entered the line of passengers disembarking.

Sondra could barely contain her impatience as they stood in line at passport control. With German efficiency, it only took them about five minutes to reach the head of the line. Speaking German, Sondra said a cheery hello the brown-uniformed, blonde man who grunted and asked for their passports. Frowning, he leafed through them slowly several times. Finally he spoke.

"Where are your vaccinations?"

"Vaccinations?" Sondra asked.

"Vaccinations for smallpox."

"We were told that American citizens don't need any!" Sondra answered indignantly.

"You were told wrong."

"Does that mean we can't go in?" Sondra faltered.

"We can vaccinate you in our clinic. Wait here on the side until everyone from your flight has finished."

"Will it take long?"

"I hope not." The man showed no emotion. "The sooner you move, the sooner I will be finished."

Sondra nodded and quickly explained to Danny what was going on.

"Do you mind getting vaccinated for smallpox?" she asked anxiously.

"I guess not," Danny answered. But he sure did not like the idea of being separated out. And to go to a German clinic, no less.

After ten minutes, all of the passengers from their flight had moved through passport control.

"Come with me," the passport official commanded as he led them to customs.

"Where is all your baggage?" the customs worker asked in heavily accented English.

"This is all we have," Sondra answered in German. "We're just here for the day."

"Open what you have," the official barked.

Danny opened his backpack first. His gemara was put on the side and his tefillin bag pulled out.

"*Was ist das*?" the worker asked.

"Excuse me."

"It's his praying strings," Sondra hastened to explain.

The worker looked at her puzzled. "It's for the camera?" He had pulled the covers off and was examining the shiny black surface.

"Please," Danny spoke awkwardly, "don't touch them."

"What are you hiding inside there?" the official scowled at them.

Suddenly Sondra remembered a picture she had seen at one of the Holocaust museums. In the foreground of the picture had been a bearded, old man wearing tefillin. Behind him were two ss officers in their brown uniforms, poking at him with their rifles and laughing. The official looked just like one of them.

You should know what they are, Sondra wanted to scream at him. *You burned enough of them.*

She swallowed the words and vowed she would not let this official see her cry. Still, tears welled up in her eyes as she faced the worker.

"Put them back. We've changed our minds. We don't want to go to Frankfort."

"You don't want to visit?" The worker was clearly puzzled by them, but the official sneered.

"I will escort you back to the international section. You can wait for your flight there."

Although Danny had not understood a word being said, he grasped that Sondra had changed her mind about going into Germany.

"Are you sure, Sondra?" he asked.

Sondra nodded silently, but once they were in the international wing, the tears overflowed and the sobs came.

"Do you want to talk about it?" Danny asked as he led her to an almost empty section in the waiting area. Gently he handed her some tissues.

She wiped her face and tightened her quivering lips.

"I felt so scared when that man in the brown uniform was going through your bag. And I knew I had done nothing wrong and that he could not hurt me, but I felt so intimidated. And then I thought about my mother and how she must have had this happen to her so many times – only so much worse – and it's no wonder she could never talk to me about it."

Sondra wiped her face again.

"Sometimes," Danny spoke slowly, "it's important to let bad memories die."

Sondra nodded. "Sometimes, though, we have to talk about them for them to die."

Danny nodded and waited patiently. It was clear to him that Sondra had something more to say.

"Danny," Sondra blew her nose and wiped her eyes again. "I never told you what happened to my cousin, Howie."

"No, you didn't."

"He was killed in a car and train accident during our last year of high school. It was a Friday night and he and the others had been drinking."

"I'm so sorry."

Danny's tone conveyed so much sympathy with just those three words that Sondra smiled weakly.

"I mourned him with the rest of the family, but, even though I never admitted it to anyone, I was angry with him, too."

"Yes." Danny prompted her carefully.

"He abandoned me for the team and the popular kids." Sondra's tears ran down her face again.

Danny waited patiently for her to regain control.

"When we were kids, in junior high, we talked about coming to Israel together and to Germany. But then, when we were older, he said those plans were just childish dreams. Going to Israel wasn't a childish dream. But I guess going to Mafdner was, even though all I wanted to do was see where my parents grew up. I wasn't even going to try and find the Torah."

"The Torah?" Danny asked as he handed her more tissues.

Sondra explained about the Torah scrolls that Kurt had rescued, Howie's bar-mitzvah speech, and their fascination with finding the missing scroll.

"I think," Danny chose his words carefully, "that by deciding to be religious and live by the words of the Torah it is as if you found the missing Torah."

"Oh, Danny," Sondra visibly relaxed as she wiped her eyes one more time, "thank you for saying that."

She looked around the lounge and saw one older woman sitting in the corner staring at them.

"Has she been here all along?" Sondra asked.

"I didn't notice 'til now," Danny admitted.

"I must look horrible." It was a statement, not a bid for a compliment.

"Go wash your face," Danny advised. "And then let's go to the El Al counter and see if we can get an earlier flight."

Chapter Thirty-Six

"*L*et's see, there's a one o'clock flight on T WA to New York, but no, that stops in London and that leg of the flight is full."

The El Al agent was doing her best to help them, but no matter how many times she turned the pages of her thick, black book, she was not able to get them on an earlier flight.

"I'm sorry. I guess the best thing is for you to wait it out. We'll start boarding a little after five."

"Thank you for your help, anyway," Danny said politely.

Sondra looked at her watch and saw they had another six hours ahead of them.

"Let's walk around the duty-free shops," she suggested. "Maybe I'll find something to read."

To Sondra's surprise, there was a nice collection of English books in the first bookstore. She and Danny looked through the shelves as if they had all the time in the world, discussing the books both of them had read.

"This was one of my favorites in high school," Danny held up *Walden* by Henry David Thoreau.

"Yes," Sondra agreed, "I liked that, too. They adapted it to a play and they did it when I was at Lincoln State. I wonder if it would still speak to me now like it did then. Did you ever read *City Boy*?"

Danny shook his head.

"You'd like it. I was hysterical when I read it. Do you want to get it?"

"You're the one who needs a book. I have my gemara."

"You may want to take a break, though," Sondra suggested. "We have a long flight ahead of us."

"Maybe." Danny held on to the book as they wandered further.

"Oh, look at this," Sondra picked up a black and red book titled *O Jerusalem*. "Did you ever read this?"

"No." Danny took the book and read the back cover. "It's about the Six-Day War."

"Excuse me," the middle-aged woman at the cash register said, clearing her throat.

Sondra looked up, ready to be reprimanded for touching so many of the books.

"If you've ever been to Jerusalem, you would probably enjoy that book." She spoke English well, although her accent was as thick as Oscar's was.

"We just came from there," Sondra smiled apprehensively.

"I thought so," the woman returned the smile. "I saw your friend's skullcap. This book describes the city so well that you feel you are there."

"Were you ever there?"

"Oh, yes," the woman nodded. "It was beautiful. The whole country was beautiful. Have you ever heard of the Yad Vashem museum?"

"Of course," Danny answered.

"Well, they planted a tree for my mother there."

"Really?" Sondra exclaimed.

The woman nodded proudly. "I went with her for the ceremony. It was one of the proudest days of her life."

Sondra could not help but relax at the warmth in the woman's voice. "What did she do during the war?"

"She hid Jews in our cellar until they could be smuggled out of the country."

"Really," Sondra caught her breath. "Where? In Frankfort?"

"No, we lived in a village not far away, Kronsfeld."

"Oh, my parents came from Mafdner."

The woman shook her head. "That was in the other direction and a long way away back then."

"Did you know what your mother was doing at the time?" Danny asked.

"Oh, yes. I was a big girl back then and I knew how to keep a secret. It was my job to take the food down to them every evening. I didn't do it in the mornings because my mother was afraid that I would be late to school and be questioned."

"Thank you." Sondra said.

The woman gave her a puzzled look.

"For telling us your story. My mother was in the camps and lost all of her family during the war. It means a lot to me to hear that there were Germans who did not hate the Jews."

"Most of the Germans did not hate the Jews," the woman said simply. "Most were just too afraid to do anything to help them."

"But your mother wasn't."

"My mother was a very brave woman and a very religious one."

"Please tell *her* thank you."

The woman shook her head. "She died three years ago, in her sleep."

"I'm glad," Sondra's voice shook a bit, "that she died peacefully."

The woman nodded and reached out to pat Sondra's shoulder. "Did you get a chance to see the museum in Blauberg?"

"Blauberg?" Sondra questioned.

"It's another small village near Kronsfeld. A friend of my mother's has a museum in her home full of abandoned Jewish artifacts. It's a shame you did not get to see it. Maybe on your next visit."

"Maybe," Sondra gave a weak smile.

"Enjoy your books," the woman spoke heartily as Danny paid and she put them in a bag.

As soon as they left the store Danny turned to Sondra.

"We still have plenty of time," he declared. "Do you want to get the shots and take a taxi to that museum? The Sefer Torah just might be there."

Sondra hesitated for only a second.

"No," she shook her head resolutely. "You were right before. I've found the missing Torah by deciding to be religious. I wish Howie could have done it with me. I wish," Sondra controlled the quiver in her voice, "that he were still here, but it was because of the dreams we dreamed together that I found the life I want to live. The life I want to live with you."